21st-Century Apprenticeship

Best Practices for Building a World-Class Workforce

Jeffrey A. Cantor

 PRAEGER™

An Imprint of ABC-CLIO, LLC
Santa Barbara, California • Denver, Colorado

Library of Congress Cataloging-in-Publication Data

Cantor, Jeffrey A.
    21st-century apprenticeship : best practices for building a world-class
workforce / Jeffrey A. Cantor.
        pages cm
    Includes bibliographical references and index.
    ISBN 978-1-4408-3418-9 (print : alk. paper) — ISBN 978-1-4408-3419-6 (e-book)
1. Apprentices—United States.   2. Apprenticeship programs.   3. Community
colleges—United States.   I. Title.
    HD4885.U5C358   2015
    331.25'9220973—dc23   2015010062

ISBN: 978-1-4408-3418-9
EISBN: 978-1-4408-3419-6

19 18 17 16 15   1 2 3 4 5

This book is also available on the World Wide Web as an eBook.
Visit www.abc-clio.com for details.

Praeger
An Imprint of ABC-CLIO, LLC

ABC-CLIO, LLC
130 Cremona Drive, P.O. Box 1911
Santa Barbara, California 93116-1911

This book is printed on acid-free paper ∞

Manufactured in the United States of America

Contents

Preface

The economic health of our nation is dependent upon a well-educated and well-trained workforce. Not since the Total Quality Management (TQM) movement has there been such a dramatic challenge to business and industry as the current skilled talent shortage. This book is about the training of our American workforce. Why? About a third of employers recently surveyed claimed that they could not find the skilled workers that they needed. Yet at the time of writing this book, about 17 million Americans were out of work, were underemployed, or worked only part-time. This dilemma is thanks in part to skill mismatches between these workers and the needs of business.

My objective in writing this book is to stimulate the interest of our nation's workforce education leadership to consider registered apprenticeship as a chosen form of proactive workforce education and training. I argue for an increased use of the concept of employer-initiated and employer-delivered apprenticeship training in cooperation with the community college.

What is registered apprenticeship? Let me begin by defining my terms. Registered apprenticeship is a formal employer-initiated and delivered training process. Throughout this book, when I refer to apprenticeship, I am referring to the U.S. Department of Labor's registered apprenticeship program—the formal process of matching potential worker as apprentice with a cooperating employer for on-the-job training in a defined skilled trade, occupation, or profession. Apprentices are employees of the firm. Apprentices perform real and productive work as they learn and master the work skills of that particular trade or occupation. It is described as a "supported journey during which an individual matures and becomes a recognized member of an occupational community."[1]

Why do I believe that we need a new vision of apprenticeship in the United States? A strong nation provides for an educated citizenry capable of growing and sustaining its businesses, its economy, culture, and way of life. My vision for new policy regarding apprenticeship stems from my belief that for America to have a world-class system for preparing a competitive and competent workforce, we must once again recognize the value of a cooperative employer-involved process of vocational training by apprenticeship. America's top 100 large-firm CEOs have expressed their beliefs that business must become more involved in preparing their workforces.

We Americans generally believe that we have such an educational system, but many of us recognize weaknesses and faults in aspects of our present systems of career and vocational–technical education that need to be addressed—and this is where, by supporting apprenticeship, community college workforce educators can make a difference.

Apprenticeship has tremendous promise for American business. Apprenticeship is the ideal method of training for the more than 48 percent of jobs in the middle-skills and high-tech occupations that will comprise the job vacancies that will exist over the next several decades of the 21st century. U.S. business, especially small business, has not fully embraced apprenticeship for its potential, and this is where the community college can make a difference. The challenge here is to enlighten and excite business and the community to explore apprenticeship as a means to join forces with adult and higher education. Together, we can train and educate workers to industry standards and produce more appropriately skilled and certified workers while concurrently supporting local economic development.

My vision of a 21st-century American apprenticeship model centers around the involvement, support, and leadership of our nation's community and technical colleges. These institutions have a long record of supporting their communities with workforce education and training. The community college has the structure and resources to recruit, assess, and match students as apprentices with local firms and employment opportunities and support the firm and apprentice with the requisite related education and training toward college degrees. It also has an exemplary ability to work in partnership to support apprenticeship with its local business and community—two essential elements for successful apprenticeship training. This is more than a philosophical issue—it is an economic issue.

The Obama administration has encouraged increased use of apprenticeship through a $100 million federal fund infusion via the American apprenticeship

Grant Program (2014) and the Community College Initiative, which is part of the Student Aid and Fiscal Responsibility Act of 2009. The administration set a goal to double the number of registered apprentices in the five years following these grants and to expand in scope past the construction trades. This federal 21st-century apprenticeship model parallels what I described and promoted in my earlier work in 1997.[2]

The book will discuss my recommendations for a 21st-century American apprenticeship system.

Acknowledgments

Researching and writing any book requires a great deal of time and, in this case, travel for research and fact-finding. I sincerely thank my wife, Ruth Cantor, for her patience and assistance in developing this manuscript. She traveled with me overseas to visit firms using apprenticeship, and she carefully edited each chapter several times. Ruth is a published author in her field and has supported my academic efforts for many decades, and I love her for it.

I also wish to thank my good friend and longtime colleague, Dr. Larry Smotroff, for providing a good and critical read of my manuscript and making very useful suggestions. Larry is very much an expert in adult education and training—his expertise is very much appreciated. I also thank my friend and colleague Lee Walker for his input and support.

Special thanks to Lukas Schoenwetter, Rolf Cavelti, and Werner Buechler of Buhler AG for their time and insights into Swiss apprenticeship and gracious hospitality in Uzwil, Switzerland.

1

A Renewed Interest in U.S. Apprenticeship

Registered apprenticeship is a formal employer-initiated and employer-delivered training process. Throughout this book, when I refer to apprenticeship, I am referring to the U.S. Department of Labor's registered apprenticeship process—the formal process of matching potential worker (apprentice) and employer.[1] Apprentices are employees of the firm. They perform real and productive work as they learn and master the work skills of a particular trade or occupation. Apprenticeship is initiated and led by a business—a firm or company—or other legitimate employer. Fuller and Unwin (2012) describe it as a "supported journey during which an individual matures and becomes a recognized member of an occupational community."[2]

Apprenticeship is a preferred method of worker vocational training in most countries around the world. A 2013 World Bank study found significant gains in the use of apprenticeship across the world's nations. In terms of percentage of each country's workforce, in formal apprenticeship in that study, Germany and Australia were at 3.7% of their workforce as compared to the United States, which was at 0.3% of its workforce in registered apprenticeship.[3] England saw a 63.5 percent growth in apprenticeship enrollment between 2009–2010 and 2010–2011 as a result of Parliament's commitment to expanding apprenticeship use.[4] In April 2013, the International Network on Innovative Apprenticeship (INAP) hosted its fifth international conference in Johannesburg, South Africa, in cooperation with the International Labor Organization (ILO), bringing together researchers, policymakers, and practitioners from thirty-four nations to discuss apprenticeship practices. Yet U.S. business, especially small business, has not fully embraced apprenticeship. As workforce development leaders, we can make a difference for our business community by promoting proactive policy for use of apprenticeship as a primary means of training and educating workers and producing more appropriately skilled and certified workers. In December 2014, the *Wall Street Journal*'s CEO council, comprising 100 chief executive officers of large companies, identified the "21st-century workforce" as its number-one priority and expressed the need for a competitive workforce—which, it suggested, requires involvement of business in the educational system.[5]

I describe my vision for a 21st-century American apprenticeship system here and explain it in the following chapters. In chapter 9, I discuss my recommendations for policy and practice as a whole.

Apprenticeship, by definition and by federal law, includes several partners. These include the firm or business employing the worker to be trained and educated in a particular occupation, trade, or craft; the worker; the governmental entity (state or federal department of labor or state department of education); and an educational entity (ideally, a community college). I will discuss the wisdom of expanding this partnership to include other community-based organizations, such as chambers of commerce, workforce innovation boards, industry associations, and the like. I will also discuss some of the more prominent and successful models used in other countries. The ultimate message I wish to impart through this book is that 21st-century American apprenticeship is a partnership of firm or business, community college, and community at large. The end result is a worker educated and trained to an industry standard for an existing job and earning a college degree along that training path.

How does apprenticeship work?   In apprenticeship, the apprentice and employer enter into a written agreement (called an indenturing or registration agreement) in a form and format prescribed by either the state government agency designated to administer formal apprenticeship (usually the state department of labor) or the U.S. Department of Labor Office of Apprenticeship. The agreement specifies the trade or craft to be learned and the length of training period. The employer provides the apprentice with a specified wage during an agreed-upon training period, which is to incrementally increase in six-month intervals as long as the apprentice meets specific training benchmarks. Herein, this "learn-and-earn" arrangement is registered or recorded with the state or federal department of labor, in turn for which the employer may benefit from certain tax incentives. The on-the-job training is conducted at the place of business in accordance with the agreement.

THE WORKFORCE AND THE 21ST-CENTURY WORLD ECONOMY

What kinds of occupations and jobs are likely to dominate the U.S. job marketplace over the next several decades? What programs are the community colleges likely to be called upon to offer? In chapter 2, I discuss the workforce and business needs for a 21st-century workforce. According to some labor economists, the "middle-skill" category or jobs, if that is a good term, will reflect about a 45–48 percent share of the U.S. labor force from 2012 to 2022. Middle-skill jobs are those jobs that require more than a high school diploma for job entry, but less than a four-year college degree.[6] These include the occupations that we rely on to keep us safe, including police officers, firefighters, and emergency medical technicians; the folks we rely on to keep our transportation viable, including automobile mechanics, truck drivers, and light rail workers; the people who build and repair our dwellings, including construction workers, carpenters, machinists, electricians, and brick masons; and essential health care workers, including registered nurses, cardiac care technicians, and radiology technicians. Such essential people that cannot be replaced by digital technology! Salaries are generally reflective of supply and demand—and demand in these middle-skills fields is high.

Apprenticeship has tremendous promise for American business. Employers in partnership with the college can train these middle-skill employees in the workplace through apprenticeship. Apprenticeship dates as far back in history as the Babylonian Code of Hammurabi. This formal training concept has existed in the United States since colonial America. George Washington was an apprentice surveyor; Ben Franklin served as an apprentice printer. Yet this is not only a historical mode of work: American apprenticeship is still used by today's businesses and employers to produce skilled workers, though not currently in significant numbers. In 2012 in the United States, there were only 375,000 indentured apprentices, mostly in the unionized construction trades. However, this represents only about 7 percent of the apprenticed workforce in Great Britain (adjusted for population size) during that same period.[7]

AMERICAN CAREER AND TECHNICAL EDUCATION IN PERSPECTIVE

Chapter 3 provides important information for the workforce development leader. Such leaders must direct their attention to the debates and discussions around issues and concerns expressed by business leaders, economists, and politicians about the shortcomings in our vocational educational systems when it comes to workforce training, including high dropout rates and faltering levels of literacy. All this results in high youth unemployment and corresponding loss of economic productivity. Those who have such concerns claim that the system produces graduates whose skills are mismatched with the needs of today's businesses and industries. From my perspective, this circumstance is exacerbated by our present American system of career and technical education, whose programs often are isolated from the needs and standards of business and industry. The net result is a loss of faith in our present system by employers as well as by the next generation of workers and their parents. Again, this adversely affects a graduate's ability to gain and maintain employment, bringing a loss of productivity and revenues on the part of the employer. All this motivates my writing of this book.

I believe that for America to have a world-class system of training for its youth and future workers, we must once again recognize the value of employers' leading the process of career and vocational training via apprenticeship to prepare a competitive and competent workforce for the middle-skills and high-tech occupations that will provide jobs over the next several decades of the 21st century. However, this employer-led apprenticeship training must be supported by community colleges and supported by other community-based organizations and educational institutions. And this is more than a philosophical issue—it is an economic issue.

Western European countries and others worldwide recognize the value of apprenticeship as a formal career and technical education process to move young people into firms when actual worker needs exist. Apprenticeship is the route to careers for more than half the new workforce of most of those countries. Twenty-four European Union member countries have formal career and technical education via apprenticeship programs. Within these countries, 3.7 million people attend apprenticeship training within participating firms.[8] Many are supported by technical schools or colleges.

As a career and technical educator, my concern is that our current system of post-secondary career and technical education is producing too many graduates whose skill sets are mismatched with what employers and the job market as a whole seek.[9] Why does this happen? I believe that career and technical education programs have dropped out of sync with business and industry needs and standards. In the case of community and technical colleges, this is not the result of ill intent, but rather because changes in industry technology and practices do not get communicated to educational institutions and faculty by advisory committee members or other communications channels quickly enough. Additionally, many community colleges are no longer able to offer a full gamut of career and technical programs due to funding constraints and slim enrollments in some of the programs.[10] Community college career and technical degree and certificate program student completer rates are well under 50 percent.[11]

What is government's appropriate role in apprenticeship? Historically, neither American entrepreneurs nor workers appreciate government involvement in the marketplace. However, government, both state and federal, plays a role and is a component in my 21st-century American apprenticeship model. The U.S. Department of Labor (DoL) (and state department of labor in twenty-five states) provides governmental oversight for the program, registering the apprenticeship agreement and periodically visiting businesses employing indentured apprentices. The state DoL ensures that the programs are operated in concert with the Fitzgerald Act and any state regulations. In South Carolina, the South Carolina Technical College System provides the administrative interface between the DoL and the firms to market apprenticeship, develop the agreement and register the apprentice with DoL, and provide periodic consultation as needed. Statistics at the time of writing indicate that there are over 375,000 apprentices in approximately 19,000 registered programs across the United States as the federal administration promotes the concept.

Chapter 3 also discusses funding incentives to firms and apprentices for registered apprenticeship. Funding for apprenticeship is also a desirable extra that the college workforce education staff can use to work with firms and businesses in their community. Some states, such as Connecticut, offer grants and tax credits to promote use of apprenticeship among firms. At the federal level, traditional job training programs to put people back to work (including through apprenticeship) are enjoying an all-time high spending level. Inclusive is the new (2014) Workforce Innovation and Opportunity Act, which places an emphasis on employer-initiated workforce training, and specifically registered apprenticeship. Funding is provided to firms through the existing system of workforce investment boards, which now take on a more prominent role of catalyzing partnerships of firms, industry consortia, and community-based organizations for workforce training, including registered apprenticeship. I will discuss how these new opportunities can be a win for registered apprenticeship.

I argue that apprenticeship programs are far different from other federally funded programs, as apprenticeship training is directly delivered inside of business and is immediate training for an existing job to which the employer has committed and that it has hired an individual to fill. Numerous states also offer tax credits and other incentives to employers and apprentices to offset registered apprenticeship costs. This important apprenticeship model dimension will be discussed in detail.

THE 21ST-CENTURY APPRENTICE

Too many of our high school–age youth are not succeeding through the educational system.   Chapter 4 is focused on the prospective worker as an apprentice. Employers are looking for skilled workers. Yet, our high school dropout and noncompletion rates are 40–50 percent in many states. Those who do graduate lack basic skills and job skills, which limits them to underemployment and unemployment. I will describe business initiatives that reach into high schools with opportunities for pre-apprenticeship. By opening the door of your business for high school youth through pre-apprenticeship programs, firms give young people an opportunity to undertake actual hands-on skills learning experiences under the mentorship and guidance of the employer. And the young person is compensated for the work. This becomes a highly motivational experience that permits part-time work to become part of the credit-earning school day.[12] Here the community college workforce education staff becomes a pivotal player in bringing prospective students (both college and high school) together with employers for apprenticeship and college dual enrollment.

Who is the apprentice?   The apprentice is a person desiring to learn a craft, trade, or profession. The apprentice is the single most important component of the model. Apprenticeship training opportunities provide a young worker with the opportunity to succeed in the workplace and develop a good work attitude, providing the unique opportunity to learn a set of industry-defined skills in an existing and available job while being paid. Usually, being an unemployed or underemployed person, the apprentice is motivated by a "learn-and-earn" opportunity. Unlike more traditional schooling, apprenticeship is a wage-earning endeavor, per the U.S. Fitzgerald Act (29 U.S.C.50). The employer will compensate the apprentice as an employee from the first day on the job at an established training wage based upon a percentage of average journeyman wages for that job title in that particular region of the country, with incremental increases—usually every six months if the apprentice meets standards for satisfactory progress on the job. This form of learning, in which reasonable wages (and perhaps other benefits) are paid, is highly desirable by most learners. Upon completion of the training, the apprentice receives a credential that is portable—recognized nationwide, if not worldwide.

During my career, I have often told parents and students that too many young people are not completing their studies and leaving school without marketable skills, including those aspiring to a community college degree or certificate—fewer than half of whom ultimately graduate. They either are not sufficiently motivated to complete the degree or have life events overtake their studies. This is unfortunate. They are most likely doomed to a life of struggle. The excuse offered by these young adults is that there are no jobs available within their communities. However, in registered apprenticeships, such young adults are training for an existing job. Again, they are employees of the firm in which they are apprenticing. This book is about the value of an age-old training process and how a new 21st-century approach can revitalize career and technical education across America. Data indicate that more than 80 percent of apprentices complete their full apprenticeship— almost three times the completion rate of the community college program rates. And the completion certificate is increasingly being accepted by community colleges for creditable advanced standing toward a college degree.

Economists and others believe that apprenticeship can be part of the solution to getting more minorities and disadvantaged learners into gainful employment. To these ends, years ago I advocated a concept termed "youth apprenticeship." A number of U.S. states now permit indenturing of youth as young as 16 in formal part-time or youth apprenticeships. Accordingly, with parental consent, high school participation, and an entrepreneur's cooperation, a young person could get vocational instruction in the workplace, with associated schooling in the subject as well as general high school curriculum, carrying over specific numbers of work hours into the regular adult apprenticeship upon high school graduation. This concept has now attracted national attention in the United States as well as worldwide.[13] I believe that consideration should be given to this concept as a regular offering in America's secondary schools.

The American public must now recognize that registered apprenticeship might be a shorter path to the American dream than a college degree alone, as a recent public television *Newshour* piece argued.[14] Parents should rethink the view that college is youths' only path to prosperity.

Workforce development leaders, take note. More than half of all available jobs during the next several decades will be in the middle-skills and high-tech fields, requiring less than a bachelor's degree, but more than a high school diploma. And these will be high-wage jobs! Registered apprenticeship can lead to a high-demand and high-skilled job and a college degree—without the burden of a college student loan. In chapter 4, I discuss these aspects of apprenticeship.

A PERSPECTIVE FOR FIRMS AND EMPLOYERS USING REGISTERED APPRENTICESHIP

To better equip workforce educators to work with business, I devote chapter 5 to the firm's perspective on registered apprenticeship. As I have visited businesses using apprenticeship and spoken with firm principals and owners, I have been both pleased and surprised to find that those who use apprenticeship do so because they find a very significant return on their up-front investment—something that should be more widely publicized in the United States. They told me that they developed their workers to suit the firm's needs and industry standards while gaining a loyal employee, fully inculcated in their corporate culture. Their existing employees also benefited by participating in the training process of the new employee. The firm also gained the services of the apprentice as that person worked and developed skills. Sixty-eight percent of those responding to a national survey indicated that apprentices contributed to a rising of the firm's productivity.

European firms also discussed the need to provide training services to their country and locale by taking on apprentices beyond their own worker needs. In Switzerland, for example, where I visited Buhler AG, it is common for larger firms to carry the responsibility of training more workers than the plant might need, as a service to the country. They also receive a government stipend for doing so.

One of the employer-expressed concerns I wish to discuss in this book is the issue of additional related education and training required for the apprentice. Apprenticeship programs require that the employer provide a minimum of 144 hours of trade-related instruction to the apprentice annually. This is off-the-job or classroom instruction related to the trade, occupation, or craft. Such instruction can be provided directly by the employer or by a recognized school or college. Many apprenticeship programs use local vocational schools or community colleges for this requirement. Of late, the desirability of providing the apprentice with an opportunity to earn a two-year or associate's degree is also an issue to be discussed. Buhler AG considers the formal school portion of the program essential to the overall development of the apprentice.

Employers tell me that the workplace is open to those who want to master a particular skill, trade, craft, or profession. Firms say that they are looking for skilled workers but can't find them. They ask about what occupations or professions are apprenticeable. Nearly every profession is apprenticeable. Economists, policymakers, and educators are now recognizing the value of the process of apprenticeship to instruction in professions and fields beyond the traditional trades. A look at the current list of over 1,500 U.S. Department of Labor–recognized apprenticeship occupations reveals titles such as public affairs worker, public health worker, and engineering and scientific programmer, among other traditional crafts titles. However, an employer can request the addition of nearly any other title.[15] In the following chapters, I elaborate upon the many benefits that accrue to an employer by training and developing its workforce through registered apprenticeship.

In chapter 5, I dispel the myths surrounding apprenticeship, discussing training costs and reported returns on investment. I will discuss recruiting of trainable talent, the U.S. process for registering apprentices and programs with the various state departments of labor, standards for training, company partnerships and consortia, additional benefits to be accrued to firms engaged in apprenticeship, and other topics of expressed interest.

A RECIPE FOR SUCCESSFUL BUSINESS AND INDUSTRY PARTNERSHIPS FOR REGISTERED APPRENTICESHIP

I have found that businesses can effectively promote and manage apprenticeships by working in partnerships with colleges and other community and industry groups, as chapter 6 will describe. Community-based organizations, state economic development agencies, chambers of commerce, trade and industry associations, business advocacy groups, joint apprenticeship councils, and consortiums of firms can assume, and have assumed, supporting roles in partnerships with formal apprenticeship. Workforce educators can help motivate these relationships. My study of European, Australian, and Canadian apprenticeship systems indicates that these groups are essential partners bridging students, employers, industry standards, and education. I will describe the rationale for such collaboration.

As a component of the 21st-century American apprenticeship model I describe, trade and industry associations are also important partners with business. I have found that international apprenticeship schemes always involve industry or trade organizations setting program standards, orienting apprentice candidates, issuing certifications, and supporting firms in delivering apprenticeship training.

The American workforce innovation board is a source of potential apprentice and a resource for funding of apprenticeship. This chapter will describe the newly legislated Workforce Innovation and Opportunity Act, as well as the workforce innovation board and how it operates. I will also discuss the joint apprenticeship training council concept that has existed for many years under the Fitzgerald Act, as well as how it operates.

Consortia of firms, usually formed in similar industries, provide many mutual benefits to the employer. Pooling of resources for outreach and recruitment, sharing of opportunities for apprentice training, arranging for related education and training through local colleges, applying for grants, and the like can be done as part of a group. I will discuss how local consortia have developed and operate, as well as how workforce educators can promote development of more of these organizations.

From an apprentice's perspective, a community-based organization as a partner is important to ensure ultimate apprenticeship program success. Throughout Europe, organizations such as the International Association for the Exchange of Students for Technical Experience (iaeste.org) and EURO Apprentice (euroapprenticeship.eu) provide help to students to match up with firms seeking apprentices as future workers.[16,17]

THE COMMUNITY COLLEGE: AN AMERICAN INNOVATION NEEDS TO BE AT THE CENTER OF THE PARTNERSHIP

I believe community colleges are an essential 21st-century American apprenticeship delivery system partner. This is a major and unique component of the 21st-century American apprenticeship model that I will advocate. As I point out to my fellow workforce educators in chapter 7, internationally, countries that have the lowest unemployment rates tout partnership between formal apprenticeship and the workplace.[18] Moreover, at the time of this writing the current federal administration has focused its thrust at expansion of registered apprenticeships in this context. Combining apprenticeship delivery with a community college degree or certificate program makes good sense in light of the advantages to the apprentice-as-learner for upward mobility with a college degree. First, our economy demands that American workers develop and keep skills current commensurate with new and emerging technologies. This requires that the worker have the general education foundations that one gains through a community college or two-year higher education. Community colleges can best accomplish this task.

The economic benefits to be derived from community college involvement in this form of business and industry training are also documentable. Lerman (2009) estimates that both the short-term and long-term earnings gains, as well as overall social benefits derived, from training through apprenticeship are significantly increased. The lifetime return on this investment is estimated as more than double the return of just a community college two-year education.[19]

The Wisconsin Technical College System (WSTC) has long provided services to businesses in Wisconsin that sponsor apprenticeships. WSTC has developed certificate and associate's degree programs to parallel the various apprenticeship programs. These programs not only satisfy the educational component requirement of the apprenticeship and provide the worker, as learner, with skills to facilitate lifelong learning, but also allow an apprentice worker's earning of a college degree. In New York, Empire State College has a long history of providing these educational opportunities to the International Brotherhood of Electrical Workers (IBEW) and other labor organizations' apprentices as students. Secondly, and as a quid pro quo, the partnership with the local firm through apprenticeship facilitates on-campus program development for the college.

Where the pre-apprenticeship segue to registered apprenticeships exists, the secondary school also becomes an important component. Many college workforce educators work in partnership with their secondary school counterparts. I discuss these arrangements as well.

Community colleges also provide access to student financial aid programs to offset the costs of tuition for the apprentice and the employer. Colleges also can provide business and industry training funding in many states to supplement any apprenticeship funding provided by the state to the business. Community colleges can provide assistance with apprentice recruitment for the firm. I will discuss exemplary dual-enrollment arrangements of registered apprenticeship and college degrees found nationwide. I will also make policy recommendations for community colleges and registered apprenticeship to further promote these arrangements.

SKILL STANDARDS AND INDUSTRY CREDENTIALS: THE FRAMEWORK FOR APPRENTICESHIP TRAINING AND PATHWAY TO COLLEGE DEGREES, DIPLOMAS, AND CERTIFICATES

National industry-designed skills standards for registered apprenticeship are an essential component that I believe needs strengthening in the United States. This is a weakness that I and others have identified, as I discuss in chapter 8. College workforce educators, take note of this model component.

What can we learn from other lands? It is important to look at other societies that have successfully practiced employer-sponsored worker training. I have looked at apprenticeship training practices and policy in Switzerland, Germany, Canada, and Australia, among other lands. I have visited Switzerland and the Buhler AG plant. In chapter 8, based on these analyses and visits, I evaluate U.S. policy and practice.

The United States has historically used a system of apprenticeship councils that are industry-created and industry-administered. Among the largest is the National Electrical Joint Apprenticeship Committee, which sets the standards for training for industrial electrician apprenticeships.[20]

The Canadian apprenticeship system, which is territorially based, has a "Red Seal" body that provides guidance and assessment for programs. Industry and firm membership permits programmatic support and a higher level of certification for the apprentice. This system is particularly attractive to me. I believe the Red Seal system offers promise as a template for the United States to consider, as I discuss later.

The United Kingdom uses a system of industry Sector Skills Councils as organizations to develop apprenticeship skills standards, certification administration, and learning policy. These organizations help match firms and potential apprentices to each other. In the UK, the Federation for Industry Sector Skills and Standards (FISSS.org) provides the interface between over half a million employers and the National Apprenticeship Service, the governmental body overseeing and funding apprenticeship. It supports eighteen Sector Skills Councils and five Sector Skills Bodies that define the skill standards for their occupations. They are responsible for defining the qualifications that together make up an apprenticeship framework. Such a framework is then used by employers to help them define the qualifications appropriate for each apprentice. In addition to establishing the occupational performance standards for training purposes, data produced by a council are also used to define recruitment practices and evaluate the incumbent worker.

It bears repeating: Apprenticeship is widely recognized and used elsewhere around the world. European countries practice apprenticeship training as part of their systems of vocational or workforce education. The International Labor Organization (2012) reviewed apprenticeship training across the G20 countries[21] and found that the benefits to a country and its economy exceed the obvious of improving employment opportunities for its workers: "Apprenticeships match the supply of skills with demand from employers much more efficiently than is possible with a system of school-based full-time vocational education" (p. 9).[22] ILO also found significant skill development when a motivated learner (apprentice) works alongside a master journeyman (employer) to develop relevant and contemporary skills while earning a respectable training wage. These higher-level skills bring more tax revenues—benefiting government and society as a whole.

TOWARD A MODEL FOR 21ST-CENTURY APPRENTICESHIP

My research for this book took me throughout the United States and into Europe looking for the best practices used in formal apprenticeship training. Based on my findings, my vision of 21st-century apprenticeship in

America consists of a number of key partners working cooperatively to produce well-trained, educated workers and community citizens. I discuss these practices, and my recommendations, in chapter 9.

Follow me through these chapters as I discuss my vision for a 21st-century American apprenticeship and describe its value to America's businesses as well as to the younger generation.

2

A 21st-Century Workforce and World Economy

This book is about embracing 21st-century American apprenticeship to adequately prepare a 21st-century American workforce in partnership with America's community and technical colleges. Too many changes have descended upon our economy and our system of higher education for us to expect that traditional systems of preparing youth for work will continue to supply American businesses with adequately trained workers. America's business leaders agree.[1] Let's look at the American economy to get a bird's-eye view of some of the changes.

America once was home to large factories employing hundreds of workers. America had both a thriving manufacturing economy as well as an agricultural economy. After becoming employed, a worker could stay with one employer until he or she was ready to retire. Any skills updating was usually arranged by the employer for the worker. Around the mid-20th century, after World War II, this began to change, and workers found themselves in a more turbulent economy requiring a change of employers two to three times over a career. The average worker in those fields experiencing the effects of technology also had to keep abreast of such changes and advances to remain employable. Today, virtually all employers must recognize the need to invest in some form of continuous training of their employees to keep and maintain a cutting-edge workforce.

THE NEW 21ST-CENTURY ECONOMY

Much change came upon the workplace with the dawn of the 21st century. Almost overnight, employers began experiencing a confluence of world competition and the need to adapt new technology to reduce overhead expenses. Such changes also caused a shrinking of the firm's workforce and an increased demand for the remaining workers to attain multiple skill sets, the better to assume consolidated jobs.

The new American economy has also witnessed adjustments to its prominent industries. Certainly manufacturing has waned as a predominant industry, but we still have a manufacturing sector presence in the United States, as well as a cleaner and higher-tech industry today. Health care has blossomed as the Baby Boomer population has aged. Information sciences has expanded and taken on new facets as America has seen a need to protect itself from the threats of terrorism. Farming and agriculture certainly reduced in size as costs to operate farms and the subsequent return-on-investment intersected. The agrosciences have reshaped themselves to incorporate elements of other industries including information technology and robotics.

Much has changed with the confluence of world community, world economy, and technology. Today, "locally produced" or "locally serviced" is becoming a thing of the past. Goods are produced worldwide—in one way or another—with some form of outsourcing along the supply chain. Kmart purchases garments manufactured in Bangladesh. Insurance companies use call centers in India or Pakistan. Your medical X-ray might be read by an MD in another part of the world. This affects how a worker is trained in terms of the degree or scope of skills within an occupation or across several occupations and the need for continuous training and retraining. Partnerships of business—even competitive firms—are now commonplace, especially within an industry supply chain.

At the time of writing, we are seeing a rebounding of production and the sale of goods and services, as well as some (but not significant) corresponding rebound in the unemployment levels across the nation. This lack of desire to hire untested and perhaps only somewhat productive workers (or multiple workers, hoping that one or two will ultimately prove useful) on the part of employers speaks to the value of a more robust system of apprenticeship in the United States. The U.S. Bureau of Labor Statistics (BLS) indicates that the U.S. economy should add 15.6 million jobs from 2012 to 2022 (a 10.8 percent increase in the labor force). Occupations that require a post-secondary level of education and training will grow faster than those occupations requiring a high school diploma or less.[2]

21ST-CENTURY OCCUPATIONS AND JOBS

What kinds of occupations and jobs are likely to dominate the U.S. job marketplace? According to some labor economists, the "middle-skill" category of jobs, if that is a good term, will reflect about a 45–48 percent share of the U.S. labor force from 2012 to 2022. Middle-skill jobs are those jobs that require more than a high school diploma for job entry, but less than a four-year college degree.[3] These include the occupations that we rely on to keep us safe—police officers, firefighters, and emergency medical technicians; the folks we rely on to keep in transit—automobile mechanics, truck drivers, light rail workers; the people that build and repair our dwellings—construction workers, carpenters, machinists, electricians, brick masons; and the very essential health care workers—registered nurses, cardiac care technicians, radiology technicians, etc. Yes, those essential people that cannot be replaced by digital technology! Salaries are generally reflective of supply and demand—and demand in these middle-skills fields is high.

The BLS projections for this family of occupations suggest very good job opportunities for this next generation of workers. Table 2.1 presents some of the BLS data showing present job numbers, projected year 2022 job numbers, percent of job growth increase, and current average salary for the job.

As the baby boom generation continues to age out of the workforce (in addition to Baby Boomers, workers 55 years old or older will constitute more than 25 percent of the labor force in 2022), the health care and social services jobs sectors are expected to grow at an annual rate of 2.6 percent, adding 5 million jobs between 2012 and 2022. This accounts for a third of the total projected increase in jobs nationally. Of the thirty occupations projected to have the largest increase in employment between 2012 and 2022, fourteen are in the health care field. Nineteen of the thirty require some form of post-secondary training. Apprenticeships to train in these areas are also growing in popularity.

We often hear about the forgotten "middle-skill worker" when listening to commentary on jobs and the economy. For that matter, even within the training and development industry, this has become a common terminology—and for good reason. Our national economy, even the world economy, cannot function without these workers. Their work is important, and the training that they receive to enter their occupations is significant, challenging, technically sophisticated, and well documented. For all of these reasons, nearly every one of these occupations is associated with a recognized certification or license.

Table 2.1 Middle-Skills Occupations for the 21st Century Growth Projections, 2012–2022*

Industry	Occupation	Employment 2012 (in thousands)	Projection 2022 (in thousands)	Percentage Projected Growth	Average Wage 2012 ($)
Health care	Dental Hygienist	192.8	256.9	33.3	70,210
	Dental & Ophthalmic Laboratory Technicians				
	Medical Appliance Technician	82.9	88.5	7	33,070
	Diagnostic Medical Sonographer	58.8	85.9	46.0	65,810
	Physical Therapist	71.4	100.7	41.0	52,160
	Occupational Therapist Aide	8.4	11.4	36.2	26,850
Construction	Carpenter	901.2	1,119.4	24.4	39,940
	Bricklayer/Mason	71.0	96.2	35.5	46,440
	Insulation Worker	28.9	42.4	46.7	39,170
Manufacturing	Line Installation Technician	249.4	267.7	7	58,210
	Machinist	476.2	510.	7	40,910
	Electrician	583.5	697.2	20	49,810
	Electromechanical Technician	17.3	18.0	4.0	51,820
Public Service	Firefighter	307	327.3	7	45,250
	Police Officer	780	821.4	5	56,980

*These data taken from the U.S. Department of Labor, Bureau of Labor Statistics, 2014.

Construction jobs are projected to grow at the rate of 2.6 percent annually over this 2012 to 2022 period. This equates to 1.6 million new jobs during this period.

The health care field has expanded significantly, with many jobs being added at the middle-skill level. This is occurring in response to changes in the health insurance industry, which is driving cost containment at the points of health care delivery. Tasks once performed by registered nurses or professional assistants are now delegated to middle-skilled technicians. Box 2.1 displays forty of the prominent and apprenticeable middle-skill health care occupations available today.[4]

Information technology is another industry cluster in which apprenticeship for middle-skill occupations is promising. Those occupations include information assurance specialist, information management IT project manager, and IT generalist, all in-demand fields.[5]

Public safety jobs will probably increase by 5–7 percent over the same time period.

Manufacturing is rebounding in the United States. Fields such as electromechanical technology are in demand and apprenticeable. In fact, as I highlight in chapter 6, apprentices are being trained in this field by firms in the North Carolina area in partnership with a business consortium formed for apprenticeship training.

What are apprenticeable occupations?   U.S. apprenticeship programs can exist in nearly any occupational area. So long as a set of industry validated worker standards can be identified to serve as the "work processes," an occupation can be added as an apprenticeable occupation. Already, more than a thousand occupations are occupationally defined on the Office of Apprenticeship's webpage (www.doleta.gov/OA/occupations.cfm). These include traditional areas such as air conditioning mechanic and some nontraditional areas (television director). A firm or business or industry group can request that additional areas be considered for addition to that list. Hereafter, I discuss occupational areas where many positions are projected to exist.

Parents, educators, high school counselors, workforce development policymakers, and the like must recognize the value of these occupations and jobs when counseling the next generation of workers. They should recognize the value of the training these workers receive when considering the merits of the occupation for college-level credit. It is accepted that nearly half the U.S. job vacancies to exist over the coming decade will require serious occupational skills that can be acquired through on-the-job training and technical education creditable toward a college degree. Yet millions of

Box 2.1

Apprenticeable Health Care Occupations

- Ambulance Attendant (EMT)
- Biomedical Equipment Technician
- Certified Nursing Assistant Lattice
- Certified Nursing Assistant I
- Certified Nursing Assistant Advanced
- Certified Nursing Assistant Geriatric
- Certified Nursing Assistant Restorative
- Certified Nursing Assistant Dementia
- Certified Nursing Assistant Mentor
- Contour Wire Specialist, Denture
- Dental Assistant
- Dental Equipment Installation and Service
- Dental Laboratory Technician
- Electromedical Equipment Repairer
- Emergency Medical Technician
- Embalmer
- Health Care Sanitary Technician
- Health Support Specialist
- Health Unit Coordinator
- Home Health Aide
- Home Health Director
- Laboratory Assistant
- Laboratory Technician

- Long-Term Care Nurse Manager
- Medical Assistant
- Medical Laboratory Technician
- Medical Secretary
- Medical Transcriptionist
- Nurse, Licensed Practical
- Optical Instrument Assembler
- Optician
- Optician (optical goods)
- Orthotics Technician
- Orthotist
- Orthodontic Technician
- Paramedic
- Pharmacist Assistant
- Pharmacy Support Lattice
- Pharmacy Service Associate Level I
- Pharmacy Support Technician Level II
- Lead Pharmacy Technician Level III
- Podiatric Assistant
- Prosthetics Technician
- Senior Housing Manager
- Surgical Technologist
- Veterinary and Laboratory Animal Technician

Source: Virtual Career Network, https://www.vcn.org/health.

vacancies go unfilled for lack of qualified workers in the United States. Registered apprenticeship has become the other four-year degree.

RETHINKING U.S. CAREER AND TECHNICAL EDUCATION

The important question for responsible citizens to think about is how we plan for tomorrow's workforce. If you are an entrepreneur, large or small, this question will determine your ultimate success. After all, unless you have a productive workforce, you will not survive.

Workforce training for a once vibrant manufacturing society came from our U.S. systems of career and technical schools and post-secondary adult training institutions. Technical colleges, community colleges, secondary and adult vocational schools, and proprietary institutes put out thousands of graduates annually, nearly all of whom obtained jobs in their chosen fields within their home communities.

What about the current supply of graduates from our nation's career and technical education system? Is it truly adequate to meet 21st-century needs? Can we continue to depend on traditional career and technical education programs to prepare our young people to succeed as part of the 21st-century workforce?

Business leaders claim that career and technical college and school-based programs are not meeting their needs and expectations. Too many students come to the job from career and technical training programs ill-prepared to demonstrate skills that add value to the firm's mission and goal. Some employers complain about a definite skill mismatch. I have heard this continually from community and technical college program advisory committees comprised of local businesspersons. Recent statistics indicate that about 34 percent of employers responding to a Manpower Group study indicate that they have difficulty hiring workers for vacancies because of a lack of qualified applicants.[6] Additionally, other studies have indicated that employers fear that the educational institution's equipment, on which students must train, is out of date. Moreover, reduced local school budgets have had a deleterious effect on career and technical education program operations, exacerbating the issue.

As an administrator, I was always concerned about my ability to continue to offer the college's entire catalog of career and technical programs. Educational programs are dependent on sufficient enrollments to be able to operate. Enrollment potential for the program is no longer predictable based on what was termed "local penetration area" population data—those populations within the college's designated service area who would likely enroll in the programs. Competing programs via the Internet proliferate, drawing enrollments away from local college programs. With the advent of online instruction, many students who might otherwise enroll in the local college or school program instead pursue studies with colleges across their states, across the nation, or even continents away via the Internet. Students are wise consumers. They will not enroll in a program if there is a possibility of the program closing or if jobs in the field are not available.

Firms today require fewer workers in any particular occupation or trade, with more broadly based skills. There is no need for fifteen to twenty construction carpenters or X-ray technicians from the local college. Students become skeptical about the employment prospects after a year or two of study and, in light of the cost of tuition, do not re-enroll in the program.

Other complaints lodged against community colleges hold that career and technical programs cannot be quickly and effectively tailored to meet local businesses' needs. The administrative processes that colleges are obliged to follow prevent them from quickly adjusting content to meet local employer requirements and demands. The college or school's ability to meet local business workforce needs becomes even more difficult if the employer modifies worker skill requirements to offset hiring costs. For instance, a local physician or clinic will hire health care assistants with multiple skills certifications, such as phlebotomist and certified nurse aide. In years past, these were two discrete workers performing either task alone, but today's worker might need to train in both skills areas to retain a job. Or a worker might come to the workplace with one set of skills and apprentice to an incumbent worker to master the second set. The net effect is that a local college might not see an opportunity to develop or modify a program if the potential enrollment for that program is low.

Within the school or college, oftentimes, a lack of program content currency is often caused by program faculty who fail to stay close enough to their industry and workplace to keep program curriculum updated. This circumstance is further exacerbated by faculty who become out of date in their occupational skills by being too long out of the workplace. Thus students come to the employer with skill mismatches that require the employer to retrain them immediately after hiring them. It is essential that the career and technical program stay current with industry-validated skills standards. Over the years, I have attempted to mitigate this issue through periodic faculty externships or sabbaticals back into local industry. This was often met with resistance and union grievances by faculty and unions, who felt this an unnecessary "punishment" of faculty who believed they were keeping their skills up to date without my help.

Often, students need a means of support during their schooling. Not only must they support themselves, but they must also sometimes support a family as well. Part-time work is one solution, but this might mean taking fewer courses and prolonging schooling. More often than not, students need remedial or developmental studies before they can pursue college-level study—even in career and occupational areas.

Prospective students are reluctant to invest time and money in higher education without a promise of a job at the end, making higher education tuition costs an issue as well. I recently heard that the average student's financial aid debt is $33,000. This alone lends support for using apprenticeship as the process for delivering career and technical skills training.

These issues have affected the ability of the community college and adult vocational education center to offer quality workforce preparatory career and technical programs.

Twenty-first-century American apprenticeship undertaken in cooperation with the employer is the most effective and efficient method for training a workforce. As posited by Lerman (2009), "Perhaps the most persuasive argument for making apprenticeship more central to U.S. skill development is the evidence that the rates of return to apprenticeship far exceed alternative training methods for middle skill jobs" (p. 13).[7] And for our government to provide incentives and tax credits for businesses to engage apprenticeship is more cost-effective than to focus funding on colleges to offer more programs.

A need for creative approaches to career and technical education.   Jacoby (2013) discusses the career and technical education dilemma in the United States. He suggests that coalitions of employers and educators can come together to promote new forms of career and technical education. New initiatives emerging include multiple forms of what is institutionalized in European countries—"dual systems" of vocational education, including internships, mentoring, programs designed to industry standards, and—yes—apprenticeships.[8] Each innovative process is designed to bring more realistic, state-of-the-industry hands-on training to students in a realistic environment.

Many U.S. community colleges do partner with local business and industry for community job training and local economic development. An example is Cuyahoga Community College (Cleveland, OH), whose president says:

> To address this important regional need, Cuyahoga Community College (Tri-C) Workforce and Economic Development Division and local business trades unions worked together to create the Joint Apprenticeship Training Committee (JATC). This comprehensive partnership helps entry level and incumbent workers enhance their skills by participating in college-sponsored apprenticeship training as

part of a credit degree program to achieve educational credentials that are vital for ongoing worker career success. (p. 10)[9]

APPRENTICESHIP AND ECONOMIC DEVELOPMENT[10,11]

Another argument for increased use of apprenticeship is its value in fostering local economic development. As an added benefit, apprenticeships are an excellent way to promote local community economic development. These two activities go hand in hand. I firmly believe now, more than ever, that economic development on a local and regional level, as well as fuller employment, depends on the mutual cooperation of community colleges and local community-based organizations, such as business collaboratives for apprenticeship, business and industry, local and state governments (e.g., departments of labor), and civic groups. However, I see the community college as the necessary catalyst for this mutual cooperation. As I said earlier, American society is becoming far too complacent in its approach to worker training and competence.

What is economic development?   Economic development is a planned and cooperative effort between the public and private sectors to improve the economic conditions in a community. The component actions and activities include the following:

a. Processes occurring within a locality or region that encourage the revitalization, expansion, and attraction of business and industry, providing increased employment activities, and maintaining or enhancing the quality of life for citizens;
b. Coordinated and cooperative efforts among business, industry, labor, and all levels of education and government (e.g., apprenticeship collaborative partnership);
c. A clearly defined role and responsibility for all groups and individuals involved in implementing the activities associated with the process.

Parties involved.   Economic development collaboration and support is often accomplished by a triangulation of business and industry; economic development agencies, including allied quasi-governmental, state, or local groups; and community colleges featuring the dual enrollment of apprentices. Figure 2.1 presents an overview of the emerging patterns of collaboration.

Collaboration in action.   I believe that economic development collaboration maximally occurs when effective and proactive cooperation

Figure 2.1   Emerging Patterns of Collaboration

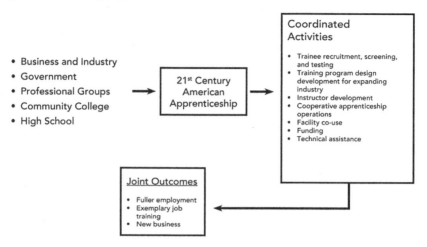

is achieved by all parties, each of whom stands to benefit in some way. Furthermore, this best occurs when it is controlled at the local level, is focused on small business, and makes best use of available resources and services without interorganizational duplication of efforts. Roles and responsibilities of each of the organizations must be clear and understood, their unique individual abilities allowed to come into play.

Business and industry role.   Local business and industry must take on a leadership role in promoting specific community economic development interests through membership on various community-based organizations, including chambers of commerce, private industry councils, councils of 100, joint apprenticeship training committees, and business associations. Activities might include working with local or state government agencies to attract new business to the locale or region, as well as working with the government to change taxing structures or to achieve other legislative actions in the best interests of the business climate. North Carolina's $50 annual apprenticeship registration fee is in legislative debate to be eliminated for deterring businesses from program use. Business and industry might also work with the local community college to train a workforce for potential business relocation or a change of production design for an existing business. In North Carolina's case, until the fee is cancelled, at least one community college partner assumes the fee for the participating businesses, helping create a condition under which proactive economic development can occur.

Economic development groups.   Again, community economic development involves a number of parties, including government agencies, business groups, and/or community economic development organizations.
State and local economic development departments provide technical
assistance and some financial resources to aid businesses seeking guidance in either expansion or relocation. Technical assistance can take the
form of site surveys or worker training guidance. Hence, assistance with
apprenticeship registration procedures, or securing of related training,
would happen here. Examples include the following:

- California's Labor and Workforce Development Agency recently
  informed California's workforce investment boards that apprenticeship
  is a priority for training California's next generation of workers and
  that state-registered apprenticeship programs will be included on the
  Eligible Training Provider Lists.
- South Carolina's Council on Competitiveness and the South Carolina
  Technical College System came together to strengthen apprenticeship
  in the state, resulting in an expansion of the automotive vehicle production industry and allied parts manufacturers.

Quasi-public agencies also are involved in the economic development
paradigm. Prominent in this category are the private industry councils
throughout the states. The Workforce Development Board of Gloucester
County (New Jersey) promotes apprenticeship and funds eligible candidates seeking to become apprentices. Likewise, the Saratoga–Warren–
Washington Counties (NY) Workforce Development System promotes
apprenticeship in upstate New York.

As a specialized not-for-profit organization, the United Association
serves as a joint apprenticeship committee helping returning U.S. armed
services veterans seek retraining through apprenticeships nationally.

THE COMMUNITY COLLEGE AND ECONOMIC DEVELOPMENT

The community college has taken on more of a local economic development role over the past several decades. This unique and very powerful
organization has the ability and capacity to serve as a catalyst in promoting overall local economic development projects. Supporting community
economic development has become part of the typical community college's mission. The college works toward this goal through its business
outreach services, such as courses for registered apprentices, customized
training for business, on-site classes and programs within business, sponsorship of small business incubators on campus or as part of the college's

community services, small business assistance centers, and so forth. Not every college engages in all these activities, and some offer more sophisticated services, such as support of business-registered apprenticeship. Let's look at how the community college can support and promote registered apprenticeship as a component part of economic development.

Technical assistance. The college reaches deep into all facets of the community for recruitment of students (including youth) as potential apprentices, provides prescreening to business criteria and skills assessment of candidate-registered apprentices, administers occupational selection and interest assessments, provides consultation in specific disciplines by college faculty to businesses as a community service, and provides general job placement services for college students to help area businesses fill general job vacancies.

Technical training. The college can provide customized training for area businesses, provide apprenticeship-related instruction, provide short courses, provide retraining or upgrade training including certification courses, provide management skills training, and provide career and vocational counseling.

Business development services. A college can provide small business incubators, partner on joint apprenticeship training councils, and provide assistance in obtaining grants and financial assistance identification.

Apprenticeship and community college dual enrollments. Collaboration between community college activities in job training and apprenticeship dual enrollment (the apprentice as an apprentice and as a candidate for a two-year college degree) and the broader economic development efforts within the community can occur in a number of ways.

Why, then, should community college leaderships consider collaboration for apprenticeship?

- Your organizations will derive mutual benefits from each other (quid pro quo).

Certainly the primary quid pro quo to be derived through interorganizational collaboration for apprenticeship is a productive job created by a firm that, in turn, allows the firm to be profitable and the new journeyman worker to enjoy a lifestyle that also adds significantly to the local economy. Hence, significant economic development happens throughout the community. To make this happen, however, the community college must recognize the benefits to itself as an organization, foremost among them the increase in the full-time equivalent (FTE) enrollment that funds the institution. The production quotient of the institution has improved through its dual enrollment of the registered apprentice. Any community college administrator should understand this argument. The firm receives the value of the registered apprentice immediately upon hire as a motivated worker producing and learning. Hopefully, the firm recognizes the long-term gain to be realized through its up-front investment in this learning experience.

Other partners, workforce investment boards, industry associations, and the like will realize their investments in long-term economic development and a fuller employment in the community.

• Community colleges, firms, and other partner organizations collaborate to increase their access to external funds.

Funding is perhaps the most motivating of the explanations for interorganizational collaboration. Funding is also the one area where we have seen the most change and improvement in the condition of U.S. registered apprenticeship. Collaboration through the joint apprenticeship training council was the initial mechanism to fund apprenticeship. Today, this is embellished through grants enabled by the community college, tax credits from the government, grants from the workforce investment council, and other sources of funding discussed in following chapters.

EFFORTS TO IMPROVE COLLABORATION FOR APPRENTICESHIP

Over the past half-decade, apprenticeship has received positive attention from economists focusing on job creation and workforce development. Part of this attention is because about 47 percent of the projected jobs over the next few decades are likely to be in the middle-skills and high technology arenas. To support these economists' prognostications, the current federal administration has focused $100 million in grant funding to promote use of registered apprenticeship, in particular in collaboration with the nation's community colleges. This partnership is designed to give young workers a path to higher education and lifelong learning, it being recognized that the new economy features fast-paced technological growth, bringing rapid changes in the nature of the workplace.

Youth apprenticeship, as an extension of the tech prep and school-to-work movements of the last several decades, is increasing in popularity. State departments of education and labor are joining together to provide supplemental grant funding to high schools, employers, and community colleges to encourage collaboration toward student-as-worker job skills development, post–high school full registered apprenticeship, and higher education pathways.

Numerous states have also put in place tax credits and other incentives to promote registered apprenticeship. I will discuss both federal and state funding initiatives in chapter 3.

3

American Career and Technical Education in Perspective

Ironically, a firm's or tradesman's taking on a helper or an employee and providing that person a period of paid apprenticeship to learn and master a trade or craft was the principal way of craft training at the dawn of our nation. Our emulation of our ancestors' method of passing on the art and science of an occupation worked very well for this nation. We were well into the 19th century before America's public schools began formal trades instruction. What happened to cause us to stray?

The years after World War I witnessed a growth of industrial trades training programs across the United States as the industrial boom created a need for significant numbers of construction trades workers and workers in allied crafts. During this period, Holmes Beckwith, a U.S. economist, attempted to promote German-style apprenticeship as the best way for America to produce well-trained workers. In his dissertation at Columbia University, he wrote, "Germany has had probably the largest and most fruitful experience of such education and has [the] most to teach us."[1] I suspect that as a proud and independent people, we resisted adopting any practice that appeared to be conceived elsewhere. The Smith–Hughes Act of 1917 marked the official beginning of a "system" of vocational education in the public schools across the United States The law was passed to address the need to reduce unemployment, reduce dependence on foreign trade schools, improve U.S. workers' wage-earning potential, and protect our national security. The next significant federal legislation for vocational education was the 1963 Vocational Education Act.

Vocational education programs across our nation produced large numbers of workers for American industry. Over time, the subjects taught mirrored the needs of a growing industrial economy. Programs developed in secondary schools, specialized vocational trades high schools, and adult training institutes.

However, although Americans resisted the movement to a dual system of education vis-à-vis the German system, American education did develop a dual path of academically oriented "college-bound" students versus "vocational students"—or "less academically inclined" students. Over time, the vocational classroom became a "dumping ground" for those youngsters who could not or would not partake of college preparatory subjects and curriculum. As a result, the instruction and learning environment in the vocational classroom suffered. The pressure placed upon parents to encourage a child to pursue a college degree, often at any cost, dissuaded young people who had good academic abilities, and who were desirous of technical studies, away from the vocational classroom. Employers drew their workforce from this supply of recent vocational school graduates (or leavers), then funded their needed on-the-job training within the business firm.[2] By the middle of the 20th century, we had developed a system of vocational education that many economists, educators, and politicians recognized as putting the defense of America at risk.

What does this all indicate for the age-old process of employer-led apprenticeship? Let's look at the historical and legislative foundation of apprenticeship in America.

APPRENTICESHIP—AMERICAN STYLE

As I have already stated, apprenticeship training is not new to the United States. In fact, apprenticeship as a means for preparing the next generation of workers predates the founding of the United States. However, with the growth in formal apprenticeship came a need for regulation. Wisconsin created the first state Registered Apprenticeship system in 1911. The National Industrial Recovery Act of 1934 (NIRA) was the first piece of federal legislation setting the stage for a national system of on-the-job training and apprenticeship. NIRA provided a mechanism for industry, trade unions, and the government to cooperate in developing a set of industry codes to govern wages, working conditions, and the quality of goods and services. On-the-job training and apprenticeship rules and regulations in the construction industry were specified.

The National Apprenticeship Act (also known as the Fitzgerald Act) (29 U.S.C. 50) followed in 1937 after U.S. Secretary of Labor Frances

Perkins led the establishment of a Federal Committee on Apprenticeship. The act and its subsequent amendments provided for a National Advisory Committee on Apprenticeship to draft rules and regulations to establish minimum standards for apprenticeship training. The U.S. Department of Labor's Employment and Training Administration administers the Fitzgerald Act. The standards governing apprenticeship programs are contained in the U.S. Code of Federal Regulations at Title 29, CFR Part 29.

The U.S. Department of Labor's Office of Apprenticeship (OA) cites government's role as follows: "The Office of Apprenticeship (OA) works in conjunction with 25 independent State Apprenticeship Agencies (SAAs) to administer the program nationally. These agencies are responsible for the following:

- Registering apprenticeship programs that meet Federal and State standards protecting the safety and welfare of apprentices;
- Issuing nationally recognized and portable Certificates of Completion to apprentices;
- Promoting the development of new programs through marketing and technical assistance;
- Assuring that all programs provide high quality training;
- Assuring that all programs produce skilled competent workers."[3]

In 2008 the Code of Federal Regulations pertaining to apprenticeship and the Fitzgerald Act was updated by Congress. The revisions included the following:[4]

- Three methods for apprentices to proceed to complete the apprenticeship:
  (1) A competency-based approach requiring the apprentice to demonstrate competency in defined subject areas and requires on-the-job training and related instruction;
  (2) Traditional apprenticeship, the traditional, time-based approach, requiring the apprentice to complete a specific number of on-the-job training and related instruction hours;
  (3) A hybrid approach, requiring the apprentice to complete a minimum number of on-the job training and related instruction hours and to demonstrate competency in defined subject areas.
- Interim credentials that enable the apprentice to demonstrate competency in specific skills and subject areas of the trade or occupation and provide portability, and that meet the needs of high-tech areas that recognize industry certifications.

- Promoting and recognizing technology-based learning that facilitates related instruction through distance learning technologies and other digital media–based modalities.

- Program performance standards that introduce completion rates as an indicator of program quality as well as existing quality assurance standards as EEO measures.

- Provisional registration, which provides sponsors with additional technical assistance in the registration process and increases quality assurance and program success rates through end-of-provisional-year program evaluation of first-time registered programs.

The Fitzgerald Act provides the foundation and regulations for U.S. apprenticeship. Federal funding support for this and other workforce training comes from a multitude of additional legislative initiatives.

Other current federal initiatives. The Workforce Innovation and Opportunity Act of 2014 (WIOA) has replaced the Workforce Investment Act as a primary federal workforce training initiative. This act recognizes registered apprenticeship as a work-based training opportunity. It fosters regional economic development initiatives. It focuses on youth programs such as youth apprenticeship. It reinforces connections to registered apprenticeship. It provides for increased reimbursement rates for employer-initiated on-the-job training and customized training. The WIOA's aim is to improve services to firms and employers by promoting work-based training. The act is designed to contribute to economic growth and business expansion by ensuring that the workforce system is job-driven (apprenticeship) through the matching of employers and individuals looking for skills training via workforce development boards. Through this act, workforce boards promote the use of industry and sector partnerships to address the workforce needs of multiple employers within an industry sector. The act provides firms and employers with increased incentives for on-the-job training including registered apprenticeship. Training that leads to industry-recognized credentials is emphasized in the act. The act also emphasizes youth and pre-apprenticeship, mandating that 20 percent of the youth formula money be spent on this activity. Clearly, registered apprenticeship wins out in this new legislation.

Workforce Opportunity Tax Credits. Employers can partake of Workforce Opportunity Tax Credits (WOTC) if they take on employees, including trainees who meet eligibility requirements for these funds. These include long-term unemployed people, recipients of public assistance under the Temporary and Needy Families (TANF) Program, disabled individuals and recipients of Vocational Rehabilitation services, and unemployed veterans. WOTC tax credits vary by category of employee (disability, TANF recipient, etc.) but could amount to a maximum of $2,400 per new employee on wages paid the first year of employment, up to a maximum of $9,000 for wages paid over the first two years of employment. For employees hired as apprentices, this could be another useful incentive to an employer.

Women's Apprenticeships and Non-traditional Occupations Act of 1992. These funds are intended to provide technical assistance to employers and organized labor to facilitate and encourage employment of women in apprenticeable jobs and nontraditional occupations. In 2012, $1.8 million in grants to consortia in six states were awarded. These were consortia of employers and local workforce investment boards (WIBs). Women still represent a very small percentage of registered apprentices in the United States.

U.S. Department of Veterans Affairs special employer incentives. The U.S. Department of Veterans Affairs also administers funding to help America's veterans return to the U.S. workforce. Veterans can receive monthly tax-free stipends to supplement their training wages in registered apprenticeship.[5] Additionally, employers of registered apprentices can receive special employer incentives (SEIs) for providing training and employment to wounded warriors and disabled veterans. These SEIs can pay up to half of a veteran's salary for six months and pay for work-related tools.[6] At the state level, several states have also put forward legislation to ensure that apprentices are protected and that the process remains sound and in accordance with federal regulations.

Certainly, the concept of apprenticeship is universally based upon partnerships. The current administration has supported the concept by placing $500 million into the 2014 Trade Adjustment Assistance and Community College and Career Training competitive grant program. This grant project focuses on partnerships of national industry associations and groups that help build job training programs through recognized industry credentials, community colleges as related education delivery agencies and career ladder support, and other community-based organizations—much like European apprenticeship. This is a great first step toward legislative funding to support apprenticeship. One of the first such industry organizations to win a U.S. Department of Labor award ($481,000) was the American Culinary Federation.

As I indicated in chapter 2, programs of career and technical education are witnessing a renewed interest among parents, young adults, entrepreneurs, educators, and politicians attempting to pose solutions to unemployment and a weak economy. Workforce education is being subscribed to in increasing numbers as an alternative to purely academic subject majors. Jacoby (2013) cites National Center for Educational Statistics data that suggests that 19 percent of high school students have attained at least 3 credits in a single occupational subject and that 18 percent of adult workers have earned a postsecondary certificate of one kind or another.[7] This trend might indicate a willingness on the part of Americans to gain skills that will lead to gainful careers. And maybe these same Americans will rethink their positions and vote for legislation that affirms and strengthens workforce training policy at state and federal levels.

STATE FUNDING AND SUPPORT FOR APPRENTICESHIP

An increasing number of states have put funding initiatives and policy in place to promote business use of apprenticeship. Among these states are Arkansas, California, Connecticut, Florida, Iowa, Kansas, Louisiana, Maine, Maryland, Michigan, Minnesota, Missouri, Montana, New Jersey, Oregon, Rhode Island, South Carolina, Texas, Virginia, Washington, West Virginia, and Wisconsin. For the most part, these incentives include tax credits to business for the employment of an apprentice and reimbursement for college tuition for the apprentice for related education and training through the community college or other educational entity. Following are highlights of the incentives and tax credits afforded businesses and apprenticees around the United States.[8]

Arkansas has a youth apprenticeship program that promotes high school–age students entering a junior year work-based program that transitions to full apprenticeship upon high school graduation. This is a formal youth apprenticeship with a written agreement between employer, student, Arkansas government, and parent. The program must include a three- to five-year work plan with on-the-job supervision and culminate in the student's earning a recognized credential in a trade having demonstrated skills for work to evince employer commitment. The educational component must include the student's ultimately earning an associate's degree or college certificate or completing a full adult apprenticeship. There must be on-the-job supervision of the student by the employer and an opportunity for team-based learning. Both academic and job credentials must be earned in the program. An Arkansas employer can receive reimbursement for up to 10 percent of the annual wages paid to the student, or $2,000, whichever is less.[9] At the time of writing, the Arkansas Department of Career Education promoted this youth apprenticeship opportunity as being for the "non-college bound" student—an unfortunate choice of words indeed.[10]

California allows community colleges and apprenticeship program sponsors to enter into excess costs arrangements wherein they can receive funds in excess of the operating costs to the colleges through the State's Montoya funds.[11] California's Department of Industrial Relations and the Division of Apprenticeship Standards, along with the Labor and Workforce Development Agency issued a memorandum to all local workforce development boards requiring that they include state-registered apprenticeship programs on their eligible training provider lists, thus enabling WIA funding to these programs. It is interesting to note that of the 55,000 registered apprentices in California, annually 22,000 are in nonconstruction occupations, including firefighting and public safety. The California Firefighters Joint Apprenticeship Council promotes apprenticeship across the state's fire departments.

Connecticut's traditional apprenticeship program is supported by a tax credit that reimburses employers up to $4,800 per apprentice per year, or 50 percent of wages paid, and a maximum of $100 per related training course taken by the apprentice at one of Connecticut's adult vocational centers—not the community college system. Pre-apprentices are not included in this tax credit program. Connecticut offers that "[s]ome examples of crafts that are eligible for the Manufacturing Trades tax credit are: Machinist, Tool and Die maker, Tool and Machine Setter, Plastic Technician, Injection Molding Technician, Mold maker and in similar occupations which involve multiple work processes including the shaping of metals by machine tool equipment designed to perform cutting, grinding, milling, turning, drilling, boring, planning, hobbling, and abrading operations, and the set-up, operation, troubleshooting, repair, and maintenance of machinery used by the Manufacturing Industry."[12]

Iowa has increased funding to apprenticeship as a favored form of workforce training and economic development through a shift in the funding administration from the community colleges to the Iowa Economic Development Authority. Eighty percent of Iowa's apprentices are in non-union firms. Iowa passed legislation that its governor, Terry Branstad, touted in his 2014 Condition of the State Address:

One of the positive outgrowths of the historic capital investments made throughout our state is increased demand for jobs. Apprenticeship programs allow us to quickly and effectively train workers to meet this demand. [. . .] These programs strengthen our middle class, our businesses and our economy. Together we can further build the pipeline of skilled workers. Together we can ensure our workers have the skills they need to fill the jobs they want.[13]

This legislation will potentially triple funding for registered apprenticeship in Iowa. However, the bill will place the funding with the state's economic development authority rather than the community college system as it previously had been.

Kansas provides reimbursements under the Early Childhood Associate Apprenticeship Program to apprentices in child care and early child education for the costs of related instruction and education, including tuition, books, and fees. In other apprenticeship programs, eligible apprentices would apply through the workforce investment board. The state is also promoting high school to registered apprenticeship as a preferred route for career education.

Louisiana provides employers tax credits up to $1,000 each tax year for wages paid to apprentices. Apprentices may qualify for grants to offset the costs of related instruction, including classes taken at the local community college through application to the workforce investment board.

Maine promotes apprenticeship among its predominantly small businesses in the state. Maine's apprenticeship program is built along the school-to-work route, wherein juniors and seniors in high school may indenture to a local firm for a part-day formal work experience coupled with traditional high school studies. After high school graduation, the student is then compelled to a full year at the community college in a trade subject and another year's continuation with the indenturing employer through completion of a one-year college certificate and the department of labor trade skills certificate. The apprentice may receive up to 50 percent a year reimbursement for tuition paid for related instruction.

Maine also received a health care sector grant from the U.S. Department of Labor that included a component to develop health care apprenticeships. Maine is also attempting to develop a program for dislocated workers to segue them back into the workforce through apprenticeships (WIA funding). Maine also has an employer-matched Lifelong Learning Account system to help workers build funds to support formal lifelong learning.[14]

In 2012, the Maryland State Legislature established a task force to study the relationship of apprenticeship to economic development in Maryland. The bill required the nineteen-member task force to analyze the effectiveness of apprenticeship in other states and internationally, including among U.S. firms abroad. The task force was charged with making recommendations for improvement to Maryland's apprenticeship programs. The task force took a look at the relationship of Maryland secondary schools to apprenticeship to determine whether an expansion to registered apprenticeship in Maryland was feasible, making recommendations accordingly. As a result of the 2014 legislative session, the Maryland Legislature developed House Bill 2207, which establishes a Youth Apprenticeship Advisory Committee in the Division of Labor and Industry. The bill stipulates that the committee will evaluate the effectiveness of existing high school youth apprenticeship programs in the state, other states, and other countries. The committee will then review and identify ways to implement high school youth apprenticeship programs in the state and means through which employers and organizations can obtain grants, tax credits, and other subsidies to support establishment and operation of high school youth apprenticeship programs.[15]

Michigan has both a traditional and a youth apprenticeship program in operation. The School-to-Work Apprenticeship Program is open to high school–age (16–19-year-old) students in formally registered Department of Labor employer-based structured work programs. It affords the employer tax credits up to $2,000 annually through 50 percent reimbursement for wage-related costs. It also reimburses 100 percent of college tuition costs for high school–age students taking college courses as part of their apprenticeship experience.[16]

Rural employers in Minnesota can receive a tax credit for "interns" they employ, up to 40 percent of salaries paid, capped at $2,000 of salary paid.

Missouri sponsors a youth apprenticeship program much like those already described. The state also offers tax credits in a number of areas that parallel apprenticeship training, such as "Missouri Work" training.[17]

The New Jersey Employment and Training Commission took the lead on a statewide initiative to develop a "clearinghouse" for registered apprenticeship and higher education. Using NJ PLACE,[18] an apprentice can identify community colleges across the state that recognize a particular registered apprenticeship or certification for college credit. This initiative includes pre-negotiated agreements between community colleges (and some state four-year colleges) and selected apprenticeships and skills certifications, facilitating the transfer of up to 25 college credits toward selected degrees.

The Rhode Island apprenticeship program is a traditional program using community colleges for related instruction. In what was once a heavy manufacturing state, the influences of manufacturers' associations remain strong. The Rhode Island Employers Apprenticeship Tax Credit applies to new machine tool and plastics processes technician apprenticeships. The annual credit per apprentice for the employer is 50 percent of the wages incrementally paid for each apprentice hired that exceeds the average number hired for the prior years, or up to $4,800, whichever is less. Youth or pre-apprenticeships are not included in this legislation. Rhode Island had approximately 1,400 apprentices registered at the time of this writing.[19]

South Carolina is serious about registered apprenticeship. In South Carolina, employers can receive a tax credit of $1,000 per apprentice who works at least seven months each year in their programs, up to four years of a program. Additionally, South Carolina Lottery Assistance funding may be available to an apprentice who is also co-enrolled in a South Carolina Technical College degree, diploma, or certificate program. Workforce Innovation and Opportunity Act funding may be available for registered apprentices to cover the costs of instruction, training, or wages. Finally, South Carolina's employers may be able to reimburse themselves for up to 50 percent of approved apprenticeship training costs (not to exceed $500 per worker) under a retraining credit for existing production employees under the Enterprise Zone Retraining Credit Program.

Texas law provides employer subsidies for apprentice-related instruction taken through the local public education agency—an adult education school or community college. That local education agency serves as the fund administrator for the apprenticeship program sponsor.

Virginia has a traditional apprenticeship program. Virginia's statute permits employer reimbursement for worker retraining that promotes economic development undertaken through registered apprenticeship approved by the Virginia Apprenticeship Council (of which I served representing the Virginia Community College System).[20]

Washington, Oregon, and Montana signed a reciprocal agreement recognizing a registered apprentice in any one of these states as registered across the three states.

For tax years beginning on or after January 1, 2012, West Virginia provides tax credits to employers in the amount of two dollars per hour multiplied by the total number of hours worked during the apprenticeship program. The total tax credit may not exceed $2,000 or 50% of actual wages paid in the tax year for the apprenticeship, whichever is less.

In late 2013, Wisconsin enacted two bills affecting apprenticeship. One new law offers subsidies to employers and apprentices. Under the law, employers can receive reimbursements of up to $1,000 per apprentice of costs related to apprenticeship. The other law enhances the Wisconsin Youth Apprenticeship Program by $500,000 annually. In 2012, the program provided apprenticeship opportunities to 1,900 apprentices and 1,300 employers. Eighty-one percent of these apprentices received job offers from their employers upon graduation.

Apprenticeship program funding in the United States is sparse at best, but soon we will look to the north, to Canada, for a comparison view. However, considering the nature of the changing U.S. and world economies, economists and politicians alike agree that a more proactive approach to promoting apprenticeship is needed. Lerman (2009), an advocate for apprenticeship, sees the need for changes in federal funding policy. He argues that with 24 million persons either unemployed or underemployed, the time has come for Congress to act.[21]

Our challenge as citizens and taxpayers is to vocalize our concerns about policy for workforce education in our schools and colleges. We need to articulate our concern about lack of proactive partnership between public education and business for workforce education. What is needed is a permanent policy package that promotes business investment and involvement in workforce training. This package must recognize a firm's need to be involved in shaping the training to meet its needs and creating a realistic process that supports trainee needs during the training period. The training policy must recognize the need for the trainee to earn a recognizable and portable credential to ensure the ability to stay employed in the event that the present employer no longer needs that employee and new employment is required. We need our elected policymakers to look "across the pond" at European countries and elsewhere to see what works in business-delivered workforce education through apprenticeship.

APPRENTICESHIP—EUROPEAN STYLE

When one speaks to career educators and employers in Switzerland about career and technical education (or, in their parlance, vocational education), a different kind of image emerges. First, unlike in America, Swiss citizens look favorably upon their system of career and technical education. The majority of youth in that country select a career path directly to work from their form of secondary education. Apprenticing to a firm or business is the way of life—and not just in the construction trades. Banking, business management, public services, information technology, electronics servicing, health care, and the like are all apprenticeable occupations. At 16 years old, a youth will move into vocational training combined with secondary schooling, spending one to two days a week in school classes and the other three days at a paid job site. Depending upon the length of vocational program, a youth may complete a two-year federal Vocational Education and Training (VET) program with a certificate or, if in a three- to four-year program, a federal diploma. Approximately 30 percent of Swiss companies participate as VET training companies. Firms participate in host company networks to enable smaller firms to be able to economically participate in VET training. Professional associations and industry associations administer the standards for training and the bridge between the school and apprentice and the VET firm. The local government (called a Canton) provides the training oversight and funding. A pathway to further education, including a college degree, is also open to Swiss youth upon completion of their apprenticeship period. This is the system in many European countries, in Australia, and elsewhere.

Apprenticeship lessons from abroad.   Much can be learned from observing other peoples in other lands that also feature an open economy and free enterprise. Australia, for example, a nation of more than 22 million, currently has a vibrant economy. During 2011, Australia reported about 449,000 apprentices indentured to approximately 4,000 registered private vocational education and training (VET) providers—the rough equivalent of our community college system for these purposes. These 449,000 apprentices represented 3.7 percent of Australia's working population. Compare that to the 0.7 percent of the United States' working labor force! Our U.S. apprentices are employed for training purposes under a contract-type agreement and receive a training wage of less than 50 percent of journeyman wage (and some with benefits), with progressive increases based upon satisfactory progress. To incentivize use of apprenticeship, compensation to the employer for taking on an apprentice in Australia is $4,000 (in U.S. dollars) per apprentice—a single amount for the duration of the training, with $1,500 paid on initial signing and the balance on completion of training. The Commonwealth government also has other apprentice-directed stipends available, such as for tools and living allowances. The state and territory governments also provide some local funding to the businesses.[22]

Canada's economy, much like that of the United States, is knowledge-based. Administration of Canadian apprenticeship is done at the province or territory level. Recruitment of youth into the trades and technologies is challenging—again, like in the United States. Canada's apprenticeship program is a prime source of recruitment and training for Canadian business. Unlike in the United States, Canadian apprenticeship is usually conducted in alternating periods of on-the-job training followed by classroom education and training. The classroom period can be six to eight weeks, followed by on-the-job work. Apprenticeships are two to five years long. Canada recognizes about 300 trades and high-technical areas today (www.caf-fca.org).[23] Canadian apprenticeship has expanded faster than in the United States. For the year ending 2010, Canada reported about 327,339 registered apprenticeships. The number of apprentices partaking of related education and training has also increased to about 20.7 percent of post-secondary enrollment. This is very significant.

The Canadian government invests heavily in apprenticeship training as a form of worker training. It is reported that 80 percent of funding for employer-sponsored training in Canada goes to apprenticeship. The average spent by the national government was $1,288 (CAN) per registered apprentice. Additionally, other grant and funding incentives paid to the apprentice to support training include $2,000 (CAN) in Canadian government incentive grants for Red Seal trades and a completion grant of an additional $2,000.[24] Apprentices can deduct, for tax purposes, the costs of tools, up to $500 year. The apprentice is eligible for the Tuition Tax Credit, including for examination fees for professional exams.[25] Apprentices are also eligible for income support during training at the province level.

Employers receive benefits at the province level as well. These include an Apprenticeship Job Creation Tax Credit, $2,000 (CAN) per year for up to 2 years; an Apprenticeship Employer Signing Bonus for $2,000 for registering their firm; and an Apprenticeship Training Tax Credit up to $40,000 or 35–45 percent of the apprentice's wages and benefits for the first four years of an apprenticeship from the Ontario Province government.[26]

England's apprenticeship programs and processes have a very long history based in the guild system. Our U.S. apprenticeship system developed along the lines of the British system. Over the last decade or more, England has been developing policy and process to refine, modify, and otherwise modernize its system to better serve British employers. The National Apprenticeship Service (NAS) was instituted in 2009 and is located in the National Education and Employment Ministry. This federal agency has overall responsibility for national delivery of the 76 apprenticeship program frameworks and standards and coordinates the efforts of the 73 National Training Organizations that identify specific training frameworks and the 47 Learning and Skills Councils that fund the programs locally.[27] Government grants to training providers in England are based upon the age and circumstances of the apprentice. For example, at the Accounting Technician level, 16- to 18-year-olds are fully funded. One hundred percent of the costs are paid directly to the training provider. Nineteen- to 24-year-old apprentices' costs are paid up to 50 percent, with the training provider expected to assume the rest. Apprentices older than 25 years are covered up to 40 percent, and the 24+ match loans (2013) will replace this government match.[28,29]

German apprenticeship also has its roots in the medieval guild system of the ninth to thirteenth centuries. The apprenticeship system of training a workforce has fared well in this, the largest European economy—and the fourth largest in the world. Though some would argue that apprenticeship only serves unions and collective bargaining, only 20 percent of German workers are represented by collective bargaining and unions.[30]

At the time of writing, there were 1.5 million registered apprentices in German firms, representing 3.7 percent of the total workforce. German apprentices are considered workers, and their salaries negotiated as such. German employers assume the full costs of the apprenticeship. There are no government subsidies for apprenticeship, except that the regional government vocational schools provide the classroom portion of the apprenticeship.[31]

France, like Germany, has an apprenticeship system dating back to medieval days. However, France has an apprenticeship tax on business. France also has a regional fund to support apprenticeship in business. France also maintains a minimum monthly pay rate schedule for apprentices, based upon the apprentice's age. This apprentice wage is excluded from the social contributions tax. Related instruction (off-the-job training) is handled by private organizations, chambers of commerce and trade, etc.[32]

In Europe, the International Labor Organization (ILO) emphasizes that a government should not micromanage apprenticeship. Its role should be a facilitator and regulator, thus ensuring that all of the participating "social" partners (firm, school, labor organization, industry association) act in the common good. Regulators should minimize the bureaucracy associated with a registered or formal apprenticeship system. ILO believes that one single entity should provide regulation, promotion, and oversight. The ILO has been very active over the last several years in promoting further use of apprenticeship across the EU.[33]

THE CURRENT STATE OF U.S. APPRENTICESHIP

Given the information above, what do we know about our U.S. system for apprenticeship that can be strengthened based on comparison to successful apprenticeship in other countries?

- We lack a cohesive "system" for U.S. apprenticeship across the United States.

Though we have one federal law detailing the processes, pay scales, and working conditions required of the employer, half our states administer the law directly through their own departments of labor, education, or economic development, the others deferring to federal administration. This results in much variation in administration across the nation. Switzerland, Canada, England, and France, among other nations, administer a single national apprenticeship program (and most nations administer it at the regional or local level).

- Our state incentives, including tax credits and tuition reimbursements to employers and apprentices, vary considerably—from no incentives to South Carolina's generous package.

Most of our benchmarked countries have a mechanism in place for government-sponsored related education at no cost to employer or apprentice. Some countries, such as Canada, have more monetary incentives for both employer and apprentice to encourage apprenticeship participation by both parties.

- The United States and Canada, among other nations, provide grants and stipends at both the federal and state/provincial levels for related instruction.

England and France provide free off-the-job higher education instruction. U.S. community colleges would be more eager to participate in apprenticeship if a funding mechanism for apprenticeship-related instruction and degree credit sponsorship was available at the state level and across all states.

- We are not reaching youth early enough, via youth apprenticeship, to enlighten them to the benefits of apprenticeship and college degrees.

Most all states now have a youth apprenticeship program opportunity. However, many states have the administration of this program in their state department of education—others within their state office of apprenticeship. Little, if any, coordination exists between these administrations, exacerbating the problem of promotion of the opportunity. European apprenticeship experiences tell us that the success to their apprenticeship training results from reaching youth earlier in their career decision making.

- In the United States, the vast majority of apprenticeship training is done in the several construction trades. Only very recently have we begun to see apprenticeship used in health-related occupations. Apprenticeship is almost nonexistent beyond these fields.

Yet our counterparts elsewhere in the world use apprenticeship across the vast spectrum of occupations in their economies. Australia has industry skills councils overseeing occupations in forest works, manufacturing, electrocommunications and energy utilities, construction and property, and community services and health. Canada has 300 occupations in its Red Seal Standards Program. The Swiss program also is very similar to these two.

- U.S. industry associations vary considerably with respect to involvement with apprenticeship. Some do promulgate work processes standards that can be used for apprenticeship program design, yet in some occupations or trades, such standards are non-existent. Likewise, industry certifications vary and are not universally used as benchmarks for U.S. apprenticeship.

Switzerland, England, Germany, and other countries have systems of industry or craft associations that identify and administer work process standards to guide apprenticeship training. They view worker competency and standardization in that regard very seriously.

- The United States does not have a system of industry-based regional organizations to market apprenticeship to their communities.

Switzerland, England, and Australia, among other countries, have a regional organization or industry association to market and promote apprenticeship among youth and businesses, bringing the two together and providing an administrative operating structure. Marketing of apprenticeship opportunities, and the like, is done at this level.

- Employers in most all of the countries are solely responsible for apprentice wages but benefit from tax credits for their participation.

U.S. employers need to recognize the value of an up-front investment in employee education and training. It's really that simple!

Lerman (2009) puts forward some suggestions for policy aimed at incentivizing businesses and government to better promote apprenticeship as a choice for workforce training:[34]

- Funding for incremental subsidies to employers to expand their in-house apprenticeship programs or to start such programs.

- Monies to market apprenticeship programs by employers, employer associations, and/or the state apprenticeship agencies (departments of labor).
- Tax credits to employers at increased levels from present-day rates. Increased technical assistance from state apprenticeship agencies would also be needed to assist more businesses in getting involved and operating apprenticeships. This assistance can be based out of community colleges.

I can add to the above recommendations:

- A workforce investment board campaign centered at the national level (perhaps the National Association of Workforce Boards) to highlight and promote the involvement of workforce boards to aggressively focus attention on the use of registered apprenticeship by firms and businesses to train their workforces across all recognized professions and technical skills areas.
- Technical consultation provided to the firm by the community college, the department of labor representative, and/or the workforce board liaison to firms and businesses illustrating how a funding package (inclusive of tax credits, available subsidies, vouchers, and student grant opportunities) can offset employer costs of on-the-job training and related and degree education.

4

The 21st-Century Apprentice

My goal in writing this book is for it to serve as a catalyst, hopefully connecting firms and employers seeking skilled employees with youth in search of training for good careers. Apprenticeship is the process by which this can happen. I wish, therefore, to enlighten both employer and young person to such a match's being a win–win situation through a formal on-the-job training relationship. The community college can be the venue for both the enlightenment and the match.

Most parents and young people have long believed that the only path to career success and economic wealth is a college degree. But there is an alternative: Apprenticeship can also lead to that degree. Why not follow a path that leads to both a skilled, high-paying career and a college degree—with both paid for by your employer? No educational loan will await you on graduation!

Consider that 45 percent of new jobs in the next decade will be in the middle-skills categories, requiring more than a high school diploma but less than a four-year degree. These are good, respectable jobs and careers.

In 2008, at the height of the most recent worldwide great recession, 15 million American workers were unemployed, and another 9 million were underemployed. Several years after pronouncements that the United States was coming out of its recession, jobs remain hard to locate if job seekers do not have reasonable skills matches to the new economy's worker skills requirements.

Young people need to be more aware of the new occupational fields emerging as changes in technology and the economy intersect. Fields such as mechatronics technology—the convergence of electronics, computer science, and mechanics—in manufacturing, automotive, and other endeavors have become a high-paying demand area.[1] Other existing occupations, such as dispensing optician in the health care field, are also promising considering the aging U.S. population. Dispensing opticians can earn $33,300 a year with a two-year apprenticeship and a high school diploma. And moving toward 2022, there will be a predicted 2,390 job vacancies in this field. A young person entering the skilled workforce today through apprenticeship can expect to earn about a quarter of a million dollars more over a career span than taking a job without that level of training, according to studies conducted by Mathematica Research. These middle-skills occupations are what will keep our economy moving—and the American way of life alive. Economic statistics indicate that an apprentice's earnings a few years after completing a formal apprenticeship will be an average of six times that of a community college graduate in a like field over that same time period, making an apprenticeship route to a career along with that college degree very financially beneficial.

Let's overcome misconceptions about registered apprenticeship and the middle-skills occupations in particular. No longer are machine shops, automotive repair shops, equipment repair facilities, and the like dirty, dark, and sweaty. Today's machine tool facilities are more like computer programming laboratories. Most repair work is done in air-conditioned, sanitary facilities, as the work must be done in controlled, clean environments. Apprenticeship is a desirable training process for nearly any occupation.

Too many students graduating (or just leaving) schools and colleges with fresh academic and workforce skills are unable to secure reasonable and appropriate jobs. Yet they have amassed unimaginable debt in the process—$32,000 or more for the average student. The world has changed from the postwar boom years. A new pathway to work is very much in demand.

One might ask a young person the following questions. Do you believe, as I do, that an electrician or welder, a nurse assistant or firefighter, a day care worker or veterinary assistant performs work as essential as that performed by a lawyer or accountant? Do you have the motivation to master an occupation or career under the tutelage of a journeyman or master and earn a college degree and industry credentials along the way? Would the following list of incentives entice you, or a person entering the junior or senior year of high school, or a person just graduating from high school, to enter an apprenticeship for training?

- Having a guaranteed job after graduation
- Being reimbursed for schooling

- Earning a fair wage while in training on-the-job
- Earning benefits (medical/dental, paid holidays)
- Enjoying travel opportunities
- Earning an apprenticeship certification from the Department of Labor
- Earning an AAS degree in a field of technology
- Earning around $34,000 after program graduation

High school guidance personnel also need to realize that preparing for careers in the trade and service professions is good, gainful employment. Realistic counseling of youth is essential. For example, part of the outreach and recruitment efforts of the several apprenticeship consortia in North Carolina is working with high school guidance counselors to enlighten them to high-tech, high-wage careers and the apprenticeship/college degree process.[2] Let's make sure that the student gets the word about registered apprenticeship as the other four-year degree.

Perhaps the answer is simple, found in age-old writings. Apprenticeship was the main training process used in ancient times. Down through the ages, youth apprenticed to master craftsmen and journeymen to learn their skills. Why would this not work in today's world as well? Today, a firm's management can use apprenticeship as a training process to clone the skills and knowledge of those of the firm's best workers who are getting close to retirement.

WHO IS A POTENTIAL REGISTERED APPRENTICE?

Job training via apprenticeship can be appropriate for several groups of people:

(a) Young people in their junior or senior years of high school, transitioning from high school to the workplace, as well as recent entrants to the workforce, aged 18–25.

Often these young workers enter the workforce in an unskilled entry-level job and quickly become dissatisfied. They seek a more satisfying and better job match and perhaps a career, not just a job. The North Carolina–based Apprenticeship 2000 employer consortium specifically provides high school students an opportunity to explore various careers as well as registered apprenticeship as a mechanism to train for good existing jobs and get a college degree simultaneously. Similarly, in the health career fields, firms such as Rochester General Health System reach out to area high school communities with apprenticeship opportunities in entry-level health care occupations.

    (b) Dislocated, underemployed, or unemployed adults seeking to enter or re-enter the workforce, as well as existing workers seeking to retrain for another job.

Workforce innovation boards under the new Workforce Innovation and Opportunity Act recognize the value of on-the-job training through apprenticeship as a means of training dislocated, unemployed, or underemployed individuals for existing high-tech, high-demand occupations.

    (c) Military veterans returning from service and seeking to transition back into civilian work.

These are important groups to consider when discussing who may benefit from apprenticeship. Veterans should look into the United Association or another major labor organization or veterans association and get assistance in securing a registered apprenticeship opportunity using their veteran benefits. The workforce investment board can aid in getting into a registered apprenticeship.

    (d) Special needs workers.

Those people with physical disabilities or cognitive impairments are another group that may benefit. Apprenticeship can aid in getting those people with disabilities into gainful employment by maximizing their abilities and strengths. There are numerous occupations that are good matches to many with physical and cognitive disabilities.

    (e) Women and nontraditional workers. Apprenticeship is an ideal way for nontraditional workers to enter good occupations.

Let's look more closely at these groups.

Today's youth and younger working adults have needs and demands, some much the same as those of years past:

- They want relevancy in their studies. They need to know that there is an opportunity to use in life what they are learning in school.
- They want expediency—an education without undue replication of courses and material.

- They also need to balance life's demands and challenges with educational goals, including family demands, community activities, and social endeavors.
- They have limited financial resources and often need to earn a living at the same time as going to school.

Not all of today's youth are ready to pursue a four-year college degree. Nor do all occupations require a college degree for entry to the career. Again, around 48 percent of the career opportunities across the U.S. economy over the coming decades will be in middle-skill occupational areas, requiring a high school diploma but less than a bachelor's degree education. Furthermore, by 2020, one-third of all jobs will require not a bachelor's degree, but rather some form of post–high school education, such as an associate's degree, certificate, or an industry credential such as is gained through apprenticeship.[3] In fact, large numbers of vacancies in traditional occupations have gone unfilled owing to a lack of potential workers to fill those occupations. Manpower's 2013 Talent Shortage Survey indicates that 40 percent of U.S. employers complain about a lack of available talent in the job market.[4] One Brookings Institute study indicates that about 10 million people remain unemployed, but about 4 million jobs go unfilled due to a lack of qualified candidates. The skilled crafts command very good salaries—certainly on par with entry-level professional salaries, if not better.

Vice President Biden has discussed the administration's Registered Apprenticeship College Consortium, which includes community colleges, businesses, labor unions, and industry organizations joining together to promote paid apprenticeships and college degrees for youth.[5] These occupations include residential and commercial electricians, communications apparatus technicians, carpenters and construction trades workers, public safety workers, various kinds of health care technicians, and the like. Nearly any occupation can be apprenticeable, including law, accountancy, and business administration, if the employer so chooses. The process is not limited to middle-skills technical occupations, as we learn from Europe and elsewhere. Apprenticeship is a good route to training for existing jobs in most fields. College degrees can be part of the cooperative arrangements of firms, community colleges, and registered apprenticeship. Some employers, such as Daetwyler USA, indicate that apprentices have gone from the associate's degree in mechatronics engineering technology on to a bachelor's in engineering and moved from technician to engineer. In fact, engineers with an apprenticeship background become a very valued employee—they better understand the systems that they work on.

Some of us learn better by doing.   Yes, many people master new skills better and faster through direct application of those skills (and associated knowledge). Their best learning styles favor emulating the master. They watch the skilled performer and then set out to perform those tasks under the master's watchful eye, with correction as needed. Hands-on learning makes learning the associated technical information much easier. Students who are not good "book learners" master the facts and concepts much better when they can put their hands to the work. Classroom study that is directly related to what you are doing on the job is much easier to master. This is how related instruction is designed in apprenticeship. It is often termed "just-in-time training." It is very motivating. Apprenticeship capitalizes upon this best learning style. Apprenticeship completion rates are extremely high. So, your chances of finishing and graduating to journeyman status are excellent—compared to the very low graduation rates of our nation's community colleges. Many studies have indicated that apprenticeship is the best form of learning for middle-skilled trades and occupations. A follow-up study of apprentices in Ireland found that of 7,500 apprentices who began their structured learning in 1999, 74 percent completed the program.[6]

The financial picture—a considered return on investment.   The costs of a traditional higher education have skyrocketed. At the same time, government-backed student loans are no longer easy to obtain or inexpensive to maintain. Youth today have become painfully aware of the need to proceed with caution in borrowing money for college. And, for the first time that I am aware of, that question of the worth of a college degree is raised by people in the know. Is there really a guaranteed return on investment in a traditional four-year college degree? Of course, the real answer is that it depends on the field of study. Apprenticeship, on the other hand, can be looked at as a fully paid scholarship, plus money in the pocket for the apprentice. The average cost to an employer to underwrite a four-year registered apprenticeship, including paying the apprentice's tuition for an associate's degree, is $170,000. This can be viewed as a scholarship.

Many of us know a young person who needs or wants to earn money while going to school. Registered apprenticeship provides this solution. Apprentices earn a real wage or salary, some starting at 50 percent of journeyman pay in that occupational area, from day one in the apprenticeship training. This is a progressive wage, increasing in six-month increments with successful performance on the job. Can you use employer paid benefits? Many employers also provide apprentices some benefits, including related training through schools and colleges. For unemployed or displaced workers, this is a wonderful way to retrain for an existing long-term job. An apprentice in a program that is articulated with a local community college can also apply for federal and state financial aid to compliment the wages earned on the job. Are you a veteran? Veterans can receive additional aid. This can help cover the costs of courses not covered by the employer, books and supplies, or other related expenses. Veterans can gain advanced standing in an apprenticeship program for military training received in the service. Certainly the financial benefits of taking the apprenticeship route to gainful employment beat graduating to a steep student loan debt.

The best of both worlds. The value of pursuing education and training through partnerships of apprenticeship and community college degrees makes sense when you look at the portion of two-year degree requirements that can be satisfied through completion of the apprenticeship program, bringing a significant savings in tuition for accruing credit for learning on the job—while getting paid to do it. In fact, we learn from England and Germany, among other lands, that apprenticeship study can extend beyond the traditional trades to professions at the bachelor's and master's levels as well. Students apprentice for jobs as accounting technicians and managers in Europe.

However, when balanced with the needs of a community and society, if the college degree is foundational upon a field of study where a business/community need exists, such higher education is a good investment. Some people select a major or course of study because they know someone who works in that field or because the field is appealing or glamorous. Too many students follow their parents' careers; perhaps they follow their dreams. All these courses of action, however, fail to look at the local job market. Upon program completion and graduation, students are disappointed to find no job opportunities waiting for them. And all too often, we enroll in technical or career programs in high school or community college that are really no longer industry-relevant. Sometimes we take courses or programs for jobs that are not available in our communities. Pre-apprenticeship, as we will discuss shortly, is an excellent method for a student to gain career guidance and an increased awareness.

Apprenticeship, on the other hand, is training for an existing job—the job a student was hired as an apprentice to fill. The entry requirements are not necessarily easy. Most apprenticeships require that the applicant be tested for basic skills and interviewed. Some also require the applicant to have met the "new basics" requirements (four years of English and three years of math, science, and social sciences).

Box 4.1

Apprenticeship 2000 Recruitment and Selection

North Carolina's Apprenticeship 2000 is an employer-driven registered apprenticeship program. Recruitment, testing and assessment, trial, and observation are all done by employers before ultimate selection of apprentices by individual employers.

The selection process begins when a high school junior or senior presents his or her transcript to the high school counselor, who works in direct interface with the Apprenticeship 2000 Consortium firms. High school counselors have been briefed and trained by the consortium to know what individual employers want in an apprentice. The counselor vets the credentials based on predetermined criteria, including English and math grades, an overall high school GPA of 2.5 or higher, and a good attendance and behavior history. Those who pass this first "gate" must then take a battery of tests—a technical math exam, a mechanical aptitude test, and other employment screening. Those who make it through this second level of screening are then invited to a six-week summer internship with a firm that also includes taking two courses at the participating community college— Central Piedmont Community College. From the results and experiences of this summer program, apprentices are then selected by participating firms for registered apprenticeship slots upon graduation from high school. This process can be more rigorous than applying to a college—and perhaps more rewarding as well.

Ideally, the apprentice as student will qualify on any college entry placement exam for the math and English courses that they are required to take toward most certificate- and associate-level courses. This has often been a problem in my experience, including in my research for this book. If this is not the case, the employer, college, community-based workforce preparation organization, and apprentice can develop a remedial plan for the apprentice to make up these academic deficiencies so that the apprentice can complete the degree or certificate.

Academic preparation for apprenticeship requires a good balance of the sciences, math, and language arts. I recall visiting Newport News Shipbuilding's apprenticeship school. I looked over their admissions application and noticed that a requirement for admission was completion of several years of high school math and science, and so forth. Certainly apprenticeship has as rigorous requirements for admission as do most academic and technical colleges. Likewise, the Michigan MAT2 programs and the North Carolina consortia programs both require solid high school academic preparation.

Once undergoing apprenticeship, you are learning the state-of-the-art skills—current skills, under the guidance of the masters in the field. For youth seeking careers in any number of career and technical and professional fields, registered apprenticeship combined with a college degree can also prove very fruitful. Registered apprenticeship is a viable avenue to existing jobs.

Consider Robert Lerman's (2009) findings from an analysis of Bureau of Labor Statistics (BLS) data. He found that currently apprenticeable occupations are expected to have generated 8 million job openings over the period 2006–2016 and that openings in these occupations are projected to reach 780,000 per year—a figure greater, he contends, than the number of community college associate's degree graduates (725,000) in the 2006–2007 school year (p. 30).[7] Just as in the manufacturing sector, at time of writing, there are more than 100,000 jobs going unfilled owing to a lack of available skills. BLS projects this number to jump to 875,000 by 2020, with a corresponding increase in job vacancies in health care and technology as well.

THE NEW YOUTH APPRENTICESHIP MOVEMENT—HIGH SCHOOL TO REGISTERED APPRENTICESHIP AND A COLLEGE DEGREE

Do you know someone who has a child in high school, either a junior or a senior? Pre-apprenticeship learning in the junior and senior years of high school can give a young person marketable skills, a career exploration opportunity, and possibly a head start on an adult career. Streamlining the educational process is important. If a student can begin to master career skills earlier in the process, such as while still in high school, and carry forward those credits or hours toward the ultimate credential—all the better. This is possible in a formal apprenticeship, as most state apprenticeship programs have statutory provisions for creditable pre-apprenticeship hours. As I first advocated in 1997,[8] this is a wonderful way to maximize the secondary school years, especially when so many youth have completed their required high school subjects by mid-junior year and end up wasting a year and a half of their lives.

Lerman and Pouncy also argue for a national educational policy that would introduce youth apprenticeship into public school curriculum as early as the eighth grade as a career awareness curriculum. This would be followed by a student's decision in the tenth grade whether to follow a purely academic track leading to higher education upon graduation or a formal three-year apprenticeship beginning in the junior year of high school and possibly ending at a community college.[9] This component of a "two-track" system is, of course, borrowed from Germany.

As you and I have painfully experienced, young workers (and, sometimes, not-so-young workers) need an opportunity to learn how to effectively work in groups and with others in the workplace. Perhaps this is becoming one of the more essential skills sets for a worker progressing through the second decade of the 21st century. In my college administrator role, I found in talking with employers that this was one consistent message employers had across the board. They expressed concern that students were not getting enough practice at working in groups toward a common goal. Perhaps the era of online learning and the computer has exacerbated this shortcoming. Working as an apprentice facilitates mastering of this set of skills, being a truly on-the-job experience, immersed in a workplace setting with other workers in all occupations. How can we channel more youth into apprenticeship programs and keep them in high school through graduation? As Nyhan relates, the workplace is a motivating "active learning" environment for youth who have a more practical form of intelligence—learners who typically do not perform well in traditional learning (classroom) environments and who often leave school with a sense of failure.[10] A process that provides motivation and immediate rewards is needed, and apprenticeship is such a tool.

Getting started—pre-apprenticeship.   Pre-apprenticeship is a recognized part of the U.S. Department of Labor's National Apprenticeship Program.[11] However, individual states differ in how pre-apprenticeship is structured. Connecticut does not require employers to make a post-pre-apprenticeship commitment, whereas Maine does. However, Connecticut offers employers a machine tool tax credit for such participation.

Historically, secondary school methods to address these issues have also included programs such as Tech-Prep, a U.S. Department of Education initiative of the 1990s. Tech-Prep involved partnerships of business and community and afforded a young learner an opportunity to experience, firsthand, the world of work. Another component of school-to-work programs that offered success in motivating high school graduation is registered pre-apprenticeship. At the time of this writing, the federal administration has promoted a new version of the youth apprenticeship concept through the U.S. Department of Labor and Department of Education, termed 21st-Century Youth Apprenticeship. This initiative is specifically aimed at bridging schooling and the world of work through apprenticeship in the high-tech and emerging fields of study.

The student and parents agree in a written agreement to work, whether part-time, as part of school hours, or after school hours, and possibly on vacation breaks and summers, for the employer for a specified period of time. The employer agrees in the same registering agreement to provide structured and formal training in a specified field or occupation over the specified period of time and in coordination with the school. The employer will also designate a person to serve as the journeyman/mentor to the student. Wages are regulated and, at worst, will be the minimum state wage. Finally, in the best of circumstances, the student moves into full apprenticeship on completion of the high school program and carries over hours for work skills mastered.[12] For example, the Connecticut Department of Labor recently reported that more than 90 percent of registered pre-apprentices went on to full apprenticeship on high school completion.

Further education post-apprenticeship becomes a reality for many youth who were not exemplary students in secondary school. Through on-the-job learning, they become better, more focused learners. They become more confident in their ability to meet goals and to master needed ideas and concepts.

DISPLACED AND DISLOCATED WORKERS AS APPRENTICES

The reality of the 21st-century economy and workplace is such that we are no longer likely to keep the same job and employer for our entire career span. We may be "downsized, outsourced, or reduced" at some time in our career—or we may elect to change jobs or careers. There are a number of different programs operating in local communities across the nation to bolster career retraining. At the federal level is the new 2014 Workforce Innovation and Opportunity Act. Similarly, The Workplace, Inc., a local workforce investment board in southwestern Connecticut, administers such programs. Displaced workers can get supportive assistance, including high school GED preparation, child care assistance, pre-vocational counseling, and the like, all to assist in preparing for a registered apprenticeship placement. Employers can effectively use registered apprenticeship to retrain existing employees in new areas in which trained talent is needed. Hence the employer can retain loyal workers despite their existing skill sets no longer being needed, retooling them when new workers are needed. Organizations such as The Workplace, Inc., can match prospective employers and apprenticeship candidates. The Saratoga–Warren–Washington Counties Workforce Development System (NY) and the Gloucester County (NJ) WIBs specifically promote registered apprenticeship for displaced–dislocated worker retraining. Displaced workers recently separated from the U.S. military can also receive assistance from these community-based workforce support organizations.

A DIVERSE AMERICA

We are, by far, a more diverse community than ever before. Caucasians are not the majority of the population. More Hispanic and Latino, black, and Asian young men and women are in the population and looking for employment opportunities. Employers are seeking them out. Jobs data reports indicate that young, less-educated, and unemployed people are not recovering quickly as the current recession improves. Apprenticeship is the best recruitment asset for both employer and employee.

Both a problem and a challenge that I have noticed is that although a young person may visit a local department of labor office and ask to become an apprentice, all too often the Department of Labor's response is to go out and find an employer who will be willing to take on an apprentice. This is echoed by employers. This is unacceptable and needs to change. Coalitions of business associations, chambers of commerce, colleges, and the government need to come together to promote the apprenticeship training approach.

However, if we have learned anything from a few hundred years of government oversight and regulation of American public education, it's that government must ensure that a system is in place for guaranteeing quality in American apprenticeship.

We do have some excellent models already in place in the U.S. apprenticeship milieu. I offer as evidence the International Brotherhood of Electrical Workers (IBEW) national electrical workers apprenticeship program. This five-year registered apprenticeship produces commercial electrical installation technicians. The evaluation measures associated with this program ensure the competency of the apprenticeship worker measured in six-month intervals. The apprentice is usually co-registered with a local community college toward a degree in labor studies or electrical technology and earns college degree credit based upon these documented evaluation measures. The American Council on Education has also reviewed these work-based and academic components and endorsed them for college credit.

RETURNING VETERANS—TRANSITIONING TO THE WORKFORCE

Returning armed services members can also benefit from registered apprenticeship training. Veterans benefits will cover those out-of-pocket expenses incurred by the apprentice and not covered by the employer, as discussed in a following chapter. Dedicated organizations such as the United Association provide a structure for veterans wishing to partake of registered apprenticeship to become journeymen construction workers (including plumbers, pipefitters, HVAC technicians, sprinkler technicians, and the like).[13] This information should be made known to service members getting ready to separate at the base information separation preparation sessions. I would regularly attend these to brief servicepersons about the community college programs available to them if they stayed in my town. A veteran can ask for consideration of military education and training achieved as part of the apprenticeship-related education requirements for a community college certificate or degree.[14]

SPECIAL NEEDS WORKERS

Do you know someone who is challenged with a disability and is looking for work or a change in employer or career? Registered apprenticeship might be just the program they have been looking for. In the past, a person with either a physical or cognitive disability was restricted in where he or she could go to gain workplace skills and where he or she could be employed. Programs through schools or community-based organizations included "sheltered workshops" and programs. However, with the new attitudes and funding opportunities, these student populations should now be able to come into the mainstream and participate in 21st-century American apprenticeship and reach one's full potential to succeed in the workplace.

For youth with disabilities, transition planning is a component of the youth's Individual Education Program (IEP) that is required by federal law. Although transition planning is required to be included in the youth's IEP beginning at age 16, many experts feel that the planning should begin earlier, at latest by age 14. The first step is assessing a youth's interests, aptitudes, and abilities and then planning specific activities and a course of study appropriate for the youth.

Goodwill of Greater Washington (D.C.) has offered a pre-apprenticeship readiness program for unemployed and dislocated workers desiring to enter the construction trades field. A nine-week program, this opportunity provides the students with the job readiness skills to enter a full apprenticeship.[15]

WOMEN AND NONTRADITIONAL LABORERS

Registered apprenticeship is also becoming a recognized training process for facilitating women getting into the workplace in jobs that previously were difficult for the female worker to gain access to. The Women in Apprenticeship and Non-Traditional Occupations (WANTO) grants program provided $1.8 million in incentive monies to help build a bridge for women to enter those occupations that had not been welcoming to them in the past.

COMMUNITY COLLEGES AND APPRENTICESHIP—DEGREE AND JOURNEYMAN CERTIFICATE

At the time of writing, American community and technical colleges are involved with registered apprenticeship in a number of different ways. Some colleges have no direct employer-to-college relationship. However, these colleges will review an apprentice or journeyman's structured on-the-job training work history to consider it as possibly college credit-worthy "prior learning" or "life experience." They will review the structured learning content using the American Council on Education as an assessor or using a local prior learning assessment (PLA) protocol.

Some colleges have arrangements with employers or employer associations to serve as the related education and training provider. Accordingly, either through their noncredit (adult education) division or their academic course division, they enroll apprentices in coursework after their work hours. The apprentice can therefore earn both credits for the workplace learning through PLA assessments and credits for the related education and training (shop math, applied science, technical courses in their trade subjects, history, and so forth).

The third scenario for community and technical colleges is to fully administer and support employer apprenticeship programs. Wisconsin's community technical colleges have long experience in apprenticeship program support. As I outlined in my earlier work, the sixteen Wisconsin Technical Colleges have a staff member at each college working to recruit and register apprentice students through the Department of Labor, processing apprentices as students and supporting related education and training throughout the apprenticeship years.[16] I will discuss this in more detail in another chapter.

Not all college degrees require four years (or even two years) of classroom attendance. Numerous accredited colleges are designed to accommodate adults' and lifelong learners' life and work experiences that parallel college-level coursework. These life and work experiences are then equated to college credit. I will discuss this further as it relates to apprenticeship experience and college degrees.

The International Brotherhood of Electrical Workers (IBEW) locals in New York have had a long-term relationship with Empire State College wherein the apprentice attends college in the after-work hours to satisfy the related training requirement of the apprenticeship, and earns college degree credit toward an AAS, then a BS. The Wisconsin Technical Colleges have similar arrangements with Ocean Spray Cranberry Company and many others.

THE STUDENT AND LIFELONG LEARNING

How does the registered apprentice take previous life experience, industry certifications earned, and apprenticeship experience to a college to apply toward a degree? The American Council on Education (ACE) is an organization that exists to "bridge" the worlds of work and lifelong learning and higher education. ACE has developed a process that is endorsed by regional higher education accreditors and colleges and universities for formally evaluating workplace training and documented life experiences for their equivalents in higher education. Apprenticeship is one of the areas that ACE has reviewed and endorsed. The International Brotherhood of Electrical Workers' electrical installation five-year apprenticeship is recognized and endorsed by ACE for college credit. The on-the-job portion of the program is rated for college credit at the first two years of a degree (AAS)—and, in fact, many colleges award the full technical major portion of a two-year degree credit toward completion of the OJT portion of the apprenticeship. This is a major motivator for a student desiring to complete a degree and learn a trade.

A NEED FOR PORTABLE CREDENTIALS

Today's workers like the ability to move from employer to employer and place to place, making a portable skills credential essential. And this is what registered apprenticeship programs provide. Under the Fitzgerald Act, apprentices who complete the registered program with an employer earn a journeyman credential in that trade or occupation that is fully recognized anywhere in the United States—being as recognizable, in fact, as a college degree granted by an accredited college or university.

The challenge today is to market registered apprenticeship more adequately to young workers and businesses alike as a viable avenue to a career path. The challenge involves incentivizing the process for firms so as to maximize their budget outlays for hiring and training a workforce. It involves providing the technical assistance to more community college systems to understand how to build bridges and partnerships to local business and industry as South Carolina, Wisconsin, and a few other states have done.

POLICY SUGGESTIONS EMERGE

My suggestions for policy consideration for increased choice of career education and training through registered apprenticeship follow:

- Promotion of youth or pre-apprenticeship through more aggressive outreach into the nation's secondary schools.

State boards of education and the various state education departments must promote and market partnerships of local business and secondary schools for career education and training through youth apprenticeship to local education agency administration. Funding made available by these state education departments must reflect registered pre-apprenticeship as a priority for career education and training.

Likewise, national organizations such as the National School Boards Association must recognize the benefits of registered apprenticeship and pre-apprenticeship or youth apprenticeship linking to adult apprenticeship, promoting this to members at the local school board level.

- Promotion of adult registered apprenticeship as a career path after high school also needs to improve nationwide.

School counselors and parents both must recognize the value of formal on-the-job training through registered apprenticeship as a desirable and viable career path to a secure profession and occupation without the burden of college loans upon program completion. Both counselors and parents need to recognize that registered apprenticeship can be done in combination with matriculation toward an associate's degree and paid for by either the employer or financial grants.

- Chambers of commerce, business, business and industry associations, and state economic development agencies or organizations need to create more visibility about the virtues of registered apprenticeship as a viable and desirable career path.

Registered apprenticeship is an economic development tool as well as an effective worker training process. That being the case, local economic development organizations must take the lead in getting out the word about the value of registered apprenticeship for preparing the next generation of workers.

5

A Perspective from Firms and Employers Using Registered Apprenticeship

A flashback to the days of colonial America would see a small firm taking on a young person as a worker and then proceeding to train that worker in the ways of the firm and the job to be done. Or a master craftsperson would train his child to be a master in that craft. The age-old system of apprenticing to learn a trade or craft was alive and well. It worked in every trade or occupation from blacksmith to lawyer (remember Abe Lincoln?).

Well, we are in the 21st century and much about American business and industry has changed. Our workforce is rapidly aging, and many skilled workers are leaving the job. Those firms that have not developed a plan for growing the next generation of workers are quickly finding themselves in need of a way to quickly acquire new talent and skills. We are also now in a global economy, and we need new kinds of specialized skills sets to effectively compete in a world marketplace.

The good news is that for a firm that has trained workers by apprenticeship, the feedback is good. By a vast margin, employers are satisfied with the process. What have I heard from a cross section of those employers (small, medium, and large) about the benefits of employing and training an apprentice? Employers (termed "sponsors" in the parlance of apprenticeship) who have engaged in apprenticeship training overwhelmingly report very positive experiences and outcomes.

For example, Lerman et al. (2009) report on the outcomes of a U.S. Department of Labor survey of 974 sponsors/employers. Ninety-seven percent of the respondents said they would recommend apprenticeship to other employers based on their experiences. Eighty percent responded that apprenticeship training helped them meet their needs for skilled workers. Comments included that a "homegrown" employee was a better employee, being more productive, making fewer mistakes, and being a better fit for the firm by bringing better customer relations skills and stronger health and safety attitudes. A noteworthy survey finding was that 68 percent responded that the benefits of apprenticeship training included raising productivity, strengthening worker morale and pride, and improving worker safety.[1] AMERITECH Die and Mold Inc., of North Carolina, feels so strongly about apprenticeship as a means of preparing its workers that on its webpage it states: "The very heart and soul of a young, vibrant, energetic group of people became the cornerstone to be able to grow the company while giving the 'toolmaker of tomorrow' the ability to learn the trade."[2]

How has apprenticeship training addressed those workforce issues faced by American business? Let's look at some of the concerns expressed by today's businesses, especially small businesses. Workforce educators and policymakers who understand the concerns of businesspersons can then best work to help overcome those concerns.

- *I can't find employees with the skill sets that I need for my business.*

This is a constant complaint voiced by business operators across America today. Small manufacturers from southeastern Pennsylvania to Fort Lauderdale, Florida, expressed concerns to me that they could not find machine tool operators and turned to growing their own through apprenticeship. Olinsky and Ayres (2013) report on a Manpower Group survey finding that 48 percent of employers have had a hard time filling jobs because worker candidates lack appropriate job competencies. This is further underscored by a Deloit (2011) survey in which two-thirds of American manufacturers reported moderate to severe difficulty finding qualified workers.[3]

The primary source of new apprentices today is an existing employee who shows promise and who is willing to be trained to a higher or more technical skill level. In the absence of this possibility, many employers turn to their local community colleges and high school partnerships to recruit either a student out of the college or a youth apprentice from the high school.

Employers do indicate a need for help finding and screening apprentices and identifying appropriate related education and training. They also want to know more about competency-based approaches to apprenticeship. The three separate North Carolina business consortia for apprenticeship training (NCTAP; Apprenticeship 2000; Apprenticeship Catawba) work collectively with their respective area secondary schools and community colleges to recruit and screen applicants for their openings. The community college is a good choice for such assistance, as has been demonstrated by the South Carolina legislature, which charged the South Carolina Technical College System to do just that. Each South Carolina technical college is staffed with people dedicated to helping businesses adopt and use apprenticeship as a training process.

- *I need to plan for the future.*

According to Jacoby (2013) only 20 percent of American employers believe that it is their responsibility to train workers.[4] However, developing and growing one's own workers through registered apprenticeship ensures business continuity. Through registered apprenticeship, the firm's owners or leaders are "cloning" the best of existing employee skills into tomorrow's employees. Planning for tomorrow's workers today is the best insurance of business continuity in a competitive marketplace. Yet Olinsky and Ayres indicate that 74 percent of manufacturers indicated that employee shortages or inadequate talent were limiting expansion of the firm or increased productivity of the firm. Hence homegrown employees become the solution for "best skills match" to the job requirements. The American business mindset needs to consider investment in the future of the business today. All too often, we only consider immediate profit and today's bottom line—but this will not work anymore, as expressed by Howard Schultz, CEO of Starbucks.

Firms such as Buhler AG, BLUM USA, Daetwyler USA, and AMERITECH Die and Mold in North Carolina tout registered apprenticeship as the means to ensure the next generation of skilled workers for their businesses.[5] Maintaining a cadre of apprentices in training is a major part of their business plans. AMERITECH Die and Mold has grown its firm through planned use of apprenticeship. Swiss-based Buhler AG provides training for itself and in excess of its immediate needs for its industry through apprenticeship. This is recognized as a civic responsibility in Switzerland and is rewarded with a federal stipend to offset corporate expenses (see Box 5.1).[6]

Box 5.1

Buhler AG is an international manufacturing company headquartered in Uzwil, Switzerland. It has manufacturing facilities and a presence in 140 countries. Buhler employs 10,000 workers and an additional 600 apprentices worldwide, In the United States, Buhler Aeroglide Co. is located in Cary, North Carolina, and in the Minneapolis, Minnesota, area. Buhler is privately owned.

Buhler's apprenticeship programs worldwide are Swiss-modeled programs. Buhler firmly believes that its people are the company's most important asset. It currently has between 5 percent and 6 percent of its workforce in a formal apprenticeship training program, with a goal of reaching 10 percent of its workforce in apprenticeship training.

The firm's philosophy, which is characteristic of Swiss businesses, provides apprenticeship training opportunities for as many youth as the firm can reasonably accommodate yearly. This figure is usually in excess of the firm's immediate needs. As a result, on an annual basis, only 70 percent of the apprenticeship completers will remain employed with the firm. The Swiss federal government provides a subsidy to the firm for its apprenticeship training service.

Youth begin apprenticeship training (vocational training with schooling) at ages 15–16. They enter into an employment arrangement with Buhler to train in one of Buhler's apprenticeship areas (approximately twelve fields). The apprenticeship program is generally three years long, with the apprentice learning and working on the job three days a week and off the job in school two days a week. The first year's basic education focuses on production skills. During the second year, the apprentice experiences practical training and gains project management skills. The final third year is focused on productive work and, perhaps, networking in a field experience abroad at a Buhler facility in another international location. The firm emphasizes the importance of an apprentice's developing social and people skills, teamwork being an essential work component at the firm. Buhler also uses an innovative videointeractive technology, "ClassUnlimited," that permits the in-house Buhler apprenticeship instructor to facilitate international classes with his or her apprentices in multiple locations.

Related instruction in Switzerland is provided at a regional vocational education school funded by the federal government. Apprenticeship skills standards and training program content are developed and monitored by trade/industry associations for the particular trade area. The professional association establishes the national qualifications, which form the basis for the federal exams.

Source: Swiss Confederation, Federal Department of Economic Affairs, "Vocational and Professional Education and Training in Switzerland," Bern, Switzerland, 2013; Swiss Confederation, Federal Department of Economic Affairs, "Entering the Labour Market: Report on Measures to Ease the Transition to Upper-Secondary Level," Bern, Switzerland, 2012.

• *Training employees through apprenticeship is expensive.*

Many firms I spoke to about apprenticeship reiterate this concern. Multiple years of employing an apprentice, even at the 40–50 percent of journeyman wage level, is expensive. The costs of a typical four-year apprenticeship, inclusive of apprentice wages and modest benefits, plus related training through a local community college, could range from $150,000 to $250,000. Maintaining an apprentice as a full-time employee adds up fast when factoring in indirect labor costs and some benefits. These facts are oftentimes the decision making considerations when deciding not to hire through apprenticeship. However, consider that about 70 percent of this cost is salary paid to the apprentice, for which there is some in-kind return in services. On the flip side, some sponsors indicate that the cost recovery offset could range up to 33 percent of those costs[7] through increased overall productivity of the firm, the apprentice's work value during the term of the apprenticeship, and ultimate reduced employee turnover by which apprentices become journeymen, as reported by numerous surveys of employers. British apprenticeship data indicates that an employer can recoup the up-front apprenticeship investment in three to four years.[8] Canada claims that employers benefit $1.47 for every apprentice training dollar spent.

Additionally, there are financial incentives and tax credits available to employers/sponsors of apprentices. For example, employers in South Carolina can now receive a state business tax credit of up to $1,000 per year for a maximum of four years for each apprentice employed at least seven months in a tax year. Additionally, an apprentice who qualifies for a Workforce Innovation Act voucher can use these funds for related instruction, books, supplies, and, possibly, training wages; moreover, South Carolina Lottery tuition assistance is available for eligible apprentices enrolled in a community/technical college degree, certificate, or diploma program. Additionally, enterprise zone retraining funds for employers who are retraining employees through apprenticeship are also available. Retraining credits of up to 50 percent of training costs, up to $500 per employee, can help existing industry maintain a competitive edge.[9] All these expense offsets can return nicely on investment for training an apprentice. For every $1 spent on the training program, $1.30 is returned over time, according to some statistics.

The South Carolina Chamber of Commerce Report of 2003 was done to study a potential expansion of registered apprenticeship in South Carolina. It indicated that Swiss employers spent an average of $3.4 billion on training annually, but these employers earned an average of $3.7 billion annually from the work produced by those apprentices and saved additional monies on recruiting and employee hiring expenses.[10]

Apprenticeship provides proven return on a firm's investment. Hiring apprentices is an investment in the future of the company. Forty percent of AMERITECH's workforce was acquired via apprenticeship training, which is viewed as a means of investing in the firm's future and maintaining a competitive edge.

Employers should view such an investment from a number of perspectives, including potential tax credits for a possible capital-type investment (a policy issue). Additionally, the time spent by existing journeymen workers mentoring the new hire, plus the money spent on the related instruction, whether outside the firm at a community college or vocational school or inside the firm with classroom instruction must also be considered. Keep in mind that the investment is also rewarded through the new energy and enthusiasm brought to the workplace by the young apprentices as employees.

- *What occupations are apprenticeable?*

Employers are surprised when they learn that apprenticeship is not only applicable to the traditional construction and manufacturing trades. Increasingly, allied health occupations such as clinicians, technicians, and paraprofessional occupations in these fields have been apprenticed. Medical informatics is a relatively recent field that has been apprenticed successfully. A prospective health care worker will be easy to recruit for work and training. Research has demonstrated that, for the apprentice, the increased value of training for the career via apprenticeship generally amounts to about $50,000 over the first two and a half years, compared to workers who gained similar training through a community college, with a gain of only $8,000 or less.[11] Any occupation or profession for which a detailed work processes listing and analysis can be developed is apprenticeable.

- *What are some additional benefits to training through apprenticeship?*

Develop and clone your best worker talents by training through apprenticeship. Learning the ways of the company from senior workers with proven talents improves employee morale, which has proven to ensure company loyalty and raise productivity according to almost 100 percent of employers/sponsors who have used apprenticeship.[12]

Employers also cite the increased breadth and depth of knowledge and skills attained by apprentices as a result of learning from documented masters of the trade. Additionally, today many apprentices are given the opportunity to cross-train in their trades, gaining skills in allied occupations that make them even more valuable employees. The apprentice is also provided with role models for how to work and behave in the employment environment.

Corporate culture is important, and apprenticeship provides an apprentice the opportunity to experience and master a company's unique culture. This helps breed long-term loyalty to a firm, producing immeasurable value to a firm.

Newport News Shipbuilding has been using apprenticeship in the United States since 1919. The firm recognizes the value of a company-sponsored formal training program to develop its own workers. Today the firm employs about 22,000 workers, of whom about 800 are apprentices in twenty-five different craft occupations. This is 13 percent of the firm's workforce—a testament to planning for the future and for growth. Eighty percent of those workers who began as apprentices are still with the firm ten years after completing their training. Newport News Shipbuilding also has developed agreements with area community colleges and a local university for higher education opportunities for these apprentices along with their apprenticeship training.

Apprenticeship programs afford the entire employer's workforce an opportunity to view education and training as a team effort. All workers grow through their individual roles in orienting and mentoring the new hires. All workers see the benefits of education and training. Apprentice program completer rates have proven to be very high, overall, compared to other kinds of training. One survey indicated that 84 percent of firms that train by apprenticeship retain their apprentice as a regular employee after apprenticeship.[13]

• *How does a firm decide exactly what to provide an apprentice training on?*

Apprenticeship is standards-based and structured and ensures consistent employee training. Apprentices are given the opportunity to master an industry-defined set of skills and knowledge. These skills and knowledge are contemporary, representing what is needed by the employer and industry. The employer as a sponsor will work with either or both a community college apprenticeship coordinator and department of labor apprenticeship representative to develop the training standards for the apprenticeship.

Apprentices add value to the workplace as they perform the skills and knowledge that they acquire. Skills and knowledge are additive, and the apprentice is constantly learning. Unlike in a sterile school environment, the apprentice is on the job, constantly contributing to the work effort.

Apprenticeship ensures that a firm's workers have mastered a firm's and its industry's standards and know about product and service requirements. Additionally, are there important considerations particular to a firm that an employer needs to consider?

- Are there employee skills unique to a firm or business that cannot be acquired through a school- or college-based program?
- Is knowledge or grounding in corporate culture essential to a new worker from the very onset of employment?

Large firms have also used the system to train their workers, as witnessed in the annals of such companies as Ford Motor Company. Why? A firm needed its workers to learn the craft fast and accurately. Although trade or vocational schools were fine for transmitting some basics of a craft, a vocational school could not replicate working conditions, own all possible equipment, and have up-to-date, state-of-the art craftspersons as instructors. After being out of the trade for a time, a teacher no longer possesses all the latest necessary skills and practices to impart them to students.

Employers can take note of some additional recent studies on employer reactions and feedback on apprenticeship training. Lerman's study, previously cited, found that apprenticeship is once again growing in popularity, up approximately 25 percent from 1997 to 2003 and growing significantly more with the recent federal and state incentives and promotion by the current administration. Of those employers who have hired and trained apprentices, 87 percent would and do recommend it to other employers as a means of gaining a productive workforce. They tout the process's ability to document skills acquisition, raise productivity of the firm, ensure worker safety, and promote good morale.

The ILO cites Business Europe in touting the advantages of formal registered apprenticeship:

- Staff are trained according to company requirements;
- Firms and employees become accustomed to the practice of training and integrating newcomers into the company culture and appreciating the importance of learning;
- If the source of the new apprentice is a well-equipped and up-to-date local vocational school, the apprentice brings fresh basic skills and perhaps new knowledge to the firm;
- Employing apprentices is a unique source of recruitment for the firm;

- Apprentices contribute to production;
- Apprentices contribute to the company with new energy and enthusiasm (p. 6).[14]

SO WHAT IS THE ISSUE?

Why don't businesses exclusively use apprenticeship any longer? Part of the answer is in the bureaucracy or perceived bureaucracy of registered apprenticeship. Business owners or managers do not want the government in "their business." They might operate informal apprenticeship programs within their firms, but they do not want the burden and intrusion of the government in registering apprentices.

- *Part of the answer is in a perceived notion that apprenticeship means unionizing.*

Apprenticeship and organized labor have become the same in the minds of business owners. This is because in the United States, apprenticeship was generally done in connection with trade unions. Though that might have once been so, it is no longer. Registered apprentices working in unionized firms account for fewer than 20 percent of all registered apprenticeships. Apprenticeship is not the exclusive purview of organized labor.

- *Part of the answer lies in little hiring going on across the board.*

Downsizing and resizing have caused firms to use existing employees in more creative ways to do more jobs. Fewer new employees are hired with the goal of keeping them as long-term employees, thus reducing invest-ment in them. But this downturn is reversing, and more hiring is happen-ing. In fact, nearly every labor force study indicates that skilled workers in all industries are in demand.

- *Part of the answer is in internal management practices.*

The firm's owners and management must recognize that apprenticeship training is an investment in the long-term viability of the business. It is succession planning for the firm's talent and skills base. The training pro-cess must be engineered into how the business works. If journeymen are compensated based on their work production (jobs completed, etc.) then the journeymen assigned to mentor an apprentice must be compensated for lost production time resulting from the mentoring process of the apprentice. Otherwise, it is unfair to the mentor and the program will not operate successfully.

- *But what about training an employee and losing him or her to a competitor after the apprenticeship is over?*

Only 25 percent of employers in the Lerman survey worried about this; 46 percent expressly disavowed any worry over the matter. The solution is providing the apprentice a good working environment and a competitive salary as graduation to journeyman occurs. Now there is no reason to leave. Training through registered apprenticeship has proven to reduce employee turnover (fewer than 5 percent of apprentices leave instead of becoming employees)—maybe because the apprentice as a worker is a better fit and well accepted by the other workers and firm management and thus is happier on the job. Greg Chambers of Oberg Industries indicates that the firm offers apprentices a variety of work assignments along with good benefits and treats apprentices with respect . . . and for the most part, they stay. He calls the apprentice program the company's lifeblood. Oberg Industries acquired about 4 percent of their craft workforce of 750 employees in apprenticeship.[15]

- *But government interferes in our business.*

This concern has been discussed in all of the surveys reviewed for this publication. Many employers expressed much the opposite experience. Employers with the Apprenticeship 2000 consortium in Charlotte, North Carolina, indicated that their Department of Labor representative is at every consortium meeting and is very supportive. Employers need an environment that has as little external interference as possible from government or other regulating entities. They need good support from partners such as community colleges if they choose to use them for the related instruction—and they should. Community colleges that interface among apprentice, employer, and registering agency can mitigate government interference and carry the burden of government paperwork for the employer. I did so in my community college supporting registered apprenticeship. They also need the correct balance of incentives in the forms of tuition aid from educational entities and tax credits from the government for using apprenticeship. My community college financial aid office provided this guidance to the businesses. Finally, they need ready and motivated apprentices—and we identified these students as well.[16]

- *Apprenticeship involves providing the apprentice some formal educa-tion in addition to the on-the-job commitment. Is that really necessary?*

Yes, structured classroom-related education is required. However, nearly every opinion of what will be needed in middle-skilled and high-skilled occupations over the next decades attests at least two years of higher edu-cation being needed. In the apprentice's situation, partnering with the local community college to provide this related education along with a two-year degree, certificate, or diploma will be a plus for the firm in knowledge and skills returned to it many times over. Additionally, because appren-ticeship candidates sometimes do not possess the basic academic skills prerequisite to a two-year degree, the community college is equipped to provide basic skills remediation to the apprentice. Surveys do indicate that employers want better communication with community colleges and pro-viders of related education. They also indicate issues when it comes to college flexibility of scheduling and accommodating curriculum changes to meet their technical information requirements.

The North Carolina consortium believes that the college degree is a necessary part of the apprenticeship package, both from the standpoint of growing as a well-rounded and educated worker and as a "selling point" to parents and students to attract the best young workers possible. Parents in the United States still want their kids to get a college education. As employers who wish to compete for the best young people to grow as their employees, including a college education in a recruitment package will be necessary.

The International Brotherhood of Electrical Workers and its New York City Local 3 have operated a five-and-a-half-year electrical apprentice-ship program for many decades. This apprenticeship program has a coop-erative educational agreement with the Empire State College wherein the apprentice must attend the college and matriculate for an associate's in science (AS) degree in labor studies. This degree is in addition to attending a five-year course of study in electrical theory sponsored and delivered by the Joint Industry Board of the Electrical Industry of New York. The union believes that trained and educated workers make for productive employees and good union members. The employers believe that electrical workers should be competent and comfortable in a demo-cratic society. They want workers to have critical thinking and analytical skills and to be able to advocate for themselves and their families. Fol-lowing Local 3's lead, the United Association Local 1, the New York City plumbers' union, also signed onto this mandatory degree requirement for its apprentices.

HOW DO WE GO ABOUT FINDING AND HIRING AN APPRENTICE?

Gaining access to qualified candidates to hire as apprentices is a problem or challenge expressed by employers in most all surveys, those conducted in the United States and Canada included. Forty-four percent of the Canadian Federation of Independent Business (CFIB) survey respondents indicated this problem. A firm can acquire new talent in a number of ways. The firm can hire off the street and take a chance on having made the right hiring decision. Or the firm can hire directly through advertising in school recruitment—again taking somewhat of a chance on making a good decision. However, apprenticeship is a very different process. Here, the firm makes an initial hiring decision knowing that the arrangement will be a structured development of a new talent. If the hiring is from a local community college and the apprentice is screened to employer requirements and tested and assessed for entry-level requirements, then the apprentice will bring good knowledge and basic skills to the firm. The firm will watch this talent blossom over time as the apprentice becomes a valued employee. The South Carolina technical colleges provide free consultative assistance to businesses getting started on registered apprenticeship for company training.[17]

Employer groups or associations, entities that exist to promote a group of businesses or an industry sector, also have a role to play in employee training through apprenticeship. Today, these entities have become essential advocates for business. The association, usually as a not-for-profit entity, can reach out to the community and serve as a catalyst for any number of activities in connection with apprenticeship, beginning with promotion of the training concept, recruitment of potential trainees, fund-raising for the activity, and so forth.

Hiring can happen through community-based workforce agencies such as the local department of labor or workforce investment board. However, of the Lerman-surveyed employers, only 17 percent reported using the Department of Labor as a hiring/referring source, and only 16 percent reported receiving applicants from a local Department of Labor office to their business as a potential apprentice. Seventy percent reported no interaction with WIA or Department of Labor whatsoever. Again, there are financial incentives available through the WIA and VA that should not be overlooked merely for the sake of keeping one's distance from these government/quasi-government organizations. An employer can use a local community college as the interface between these funding and support organizations and the firm.

HOW DOES AN EMPLOYER BECOME INVOLVED IN A PARTNERSHIP TO SUPPORT APPRENTICESHIP TRAINING?

Though not as prominently in the United States, successful association partnerships have developed to support forms of cooperative on-the-job learning such as apprenticeship. Local community colleges are masters at bringing together businesses, multiple educational organizations, industry groups, and governments to provide educational services through partnerships.

The South Carolina Technical College System has been out front nationally in promoting the value of registered apprenticeship delivered in cooperation and combination with the state's technical colleges. South Carolina boasts a 210 percent growth in registered apprenticeship since 2007. One such partnership involving a local technical college in Barnwell, South Carolina, Denmark Technical College, is with Horsehead Corp., a specialty provider of zinc-based products. This electromechanical technician program is a three-year registered apprenticeship, funded in part by the third partner, the state workforce investment board, and the local workforce innovation board. Each partner achieves its goals and objectives through cooperation.

Several regional consortia have developed to deliver apprenticeships in North Carolina. Among these are Apprenticeship 2000 in the Charlotte area, the North Carolina Triangle Apprenticeship Program (NCTAP) in the Raleigh–Durham area, and Apprenticeship Catawba. These consortia include businesses, small and large, a community college and area high schools, and the North Carolina state apprenticeship representative. Among the benefits to member employers, some of the firms will share training opportunities so that apprentices can gain a full and complete skills development experience. This is important in small businesses, in which the firm might not perform all the aspects or facets of a particular trade and thus an apprentice would not have an opportunity to master those missing tasks were it not for other firms inviting them in for that portion of the apprenticeship.

Some of the other industry organizations that we find in the apprenticeship milieu are outgrowths of organized labor. As mentioned earlier, the California Fire Fighter Joint Apprenticeship Committee (CFFJAC) serves multiple roles in coordinating firefighter and officer apprenticeship training. It oversees the standards underwriting the apprenticeships based on National Apprenticeship and Training Standards for the Firefighter, and it advertises and promotes apprenticeship to both fire departments and potential apprentices. It sponsors physical agility testing for apprenticeship. The CFFJAC also monitors training programs offered by participating colleges.[18]

Firefighter unions in California look to the CFFJAC as an organization that ensures equitable service to all participants. A local fire department must agree to (1) recruitment and selection of apprentices, (2) provision of training standards and processes to apprentices, (3) training period length, and (4) wages paid to apprentices, including incremental increases.

HOW DO PARTNERSHIPS SUCCEED?

As I discussed in chapter 2, over my years researching apprenticeship programs and interorganizational relationships to deliver such programs, I found three principal reasons why interorganizational relationships work to promote apprenticeship program delivery:[19]

- Organizations successfully collaborate because they derive mutual exchanges from each other;
- Organizations collaborate because they are able to increase their access to external funds;
- Organizations collaborate because they develop formal agreements between each other, specifying the responsibilities of each participating organization.

Where a quid pro quo exists and all parties come away with benefits derived from interorganizational working relationships, these relationships sustain themselves. Community college administrators who work with a trade association or employer group to provide related education and training to apprentices yields the college potential course enrollments. For the employer, working with the college in the relationship provides a source of high-quality education and training for apprentices. For the local department of labor (the government partner), both the college and employer fulfill two essential parts of the apprenticeship scheme. The burden of the official paperwork and the program oversight become the third component fulfilled by Department of Labor. However, other benefits to be derived by potential participants include community economic development through a fuller and more robust employment of citizens. Hence the economic development authority can also derive benefits from participation.

The agreement between the partners is an essential document. All community partners must know exactly what their roles and responsibilities are going to be before the partnership becomes reality. The documents creating the partnership relationship should enumerate who each partner is and the role of each. It should stipulate what resources each brings to the partnership. The document will also stipulate what each partner will glean from participation. For example, the partnership might be a training and community service partnership such as I enjoyed with the Pensacola Habitat for Humanity. Pensacola Junior College had a construction trades training program that needed a hands-on component to reinforce laboratory work done on campus. Pensacola Habitat for Humanity provided housing for people in need within the community. HH relies on volunteers for its workers. The partnership worked very well as a result of a very well-thought-through written agreement.

Funding for any program is an essential component. Interorganizational grant applicants are always far more successful than single applicants. In fact, in today's federal grants application world, multiple community partners are a requirement. Additionally, a community college as a partner provides access to federal student tuition grants, educational loans, and other private tuition grants. In the construction trades partnership example earlier mentioned, a job training agency eventually joined in providing access to federal housing job training grants to underwrite tuition for unemployed occupants of public housing in need of job training. A significant benefit to American apprenticeship is the ability for community colleges to provide access to Pell and Perkins funding vehicles to compliment an apprenticeship partnership. This is witnessed in the Wisconsin Technical College System, in which each of the WTI colleges works with apprentices to develop tuition aid packages to support student ability to complete a degree program along with an apprenticeship. When economic development agencies join the group, other kinds of community economic funding can also be explored, such as those previously discussed.

POLICY IMPLICATIONS AND RECOMMENDATIONS

What I have found through my research and observations about firms and businesses using registered apprenticeship can be formulated into the following recommendations.

- Firms need to adopt a civic spirit about participating in registered apprenticeship. Larger firms with increased production capacity might take on apprentices in excess of their immediate hiring needs to provide smaller firms with trained people to later hire. A funding initiative such as the WIOA could serve as a pool of funds to offset such expenses on the part of such firms.

- States need to consolidate the registered apprenticeship support for businesses in a single organization having universal outreach and resources within a state, such as the community college system. The South Carolina model can serve as an excellent example for this.
- Local business consortia have proven very successful supporting registered apprenticeship. The North Carolina Department of Labor has worked well to link area businesses together to facilitate replication of this model. Other state departments of labor or community college systems can follow this lead to provide a mechanism for replication.
- State economic development organizations need to better communicate the return on investment of registered apprenticeship to local and small businesses.

6

A Recipe for Successful Business and Industry Partnerships for Registered Apprenticeship: A Look at the Best of the Best

We Americans excel when it comes to working together toward a common community goal. Sometimes it's for recreation and play, sometimes to solve a civic issue or problem, and sometimes to create business and economic development. However, education and training in the United States has traditionally been carried out at schools. Business is accustomed to looking toward an educational organization for training and talent sources. Apprenticeship is a collaborative process—by its very nature a partnership of firm, apprentice, and, usually, an outside educational institution. In some instances, for the apprenticeship process to succeed, there needs to be an intermediate organization supporting the firm's endeavors. The community college best meets this role.

Many firms choose to partner with other firms, sometimes competitor firms, to deliver registered apprenticeship. The motivation for this joining of forces is generally economic. In some cases, it has to do with gaining necessary community and government resources to facilitate the apprenticeship. In writing this book, I found that businesses collaborate with each other for a number of reasons:

- They derive mutual exchanges from each other;

- They are able to increase their access to external funds;
- They develop formal agreements between each other, specifying the responsibilities of each participating organization.

Before discussing the various kinds of collaborating configurations currently in practice, a few words about other countries' approaches are in order. The Swiss have a system of sectorial organizations that provide the outreach to business and industry orientation and some technical instruction to apprentices. The Australians use a system of apprenticeship centers contracted by the federal government to provide their services. Canada's provincial governments provide the coordinating services for the Red Seal and other apprenticeships.

Registered apprenticeship is an employer-driven activity. Yes, single employers can (and do) go it alone, hiring a single apprentice or more, registering the apprenticeship with the state department of labor, and contracting for related training with a local school or community college (or delivering it within the firm). However, multiple employers can elect to come together through any number of venues—a trade group, association, or consortium—to share resources and responsibilities and participate in registered apprenticeship. Community colleges can be an effective catalyst for bringing firms and businesses together for apprenticeship program operation. In such a case, the business or trade association often designs the program and then administers the apprenticeship documentation and registration process with the state department of labor.

TRADE ASSOCIATIONS SUPPORT APPRENTICESHIP

I have found that several apprenticeship programs were begun by local trade associations because their member small manufacturing firms were having difficulties locating skilled machine tool workers. Discussions with them revealed that this situation occurred as local schools and community colleges no longer offered vocational programs, such as machine tool technology, that would produce the technical personnel they required. Accordingly, in southeast Florida, the South Florida Manufacturers' Association (SFMA) created the machinist apprenticeship program. An association staff member oversees the program administration, including apprentice registration. The staff member collaborates with the Broward County Atlantic Technical Center to provide the related training classes associated with a machinist apprenticeship program. Funding for the program comes from employer contributions to the SFMA and from related courses underwritten by the local adult education center. The program uses the National Institute for Metalworking Skills (NIMS) skills standards as the basis for its work processes standards.[1] At the time of writing, the SFMA Machinist Apprenticeship Program coordinator was in discussion with two colleges to build an articulation program to permit apprentices to use their OJT and related instruction time and certifications toward college credits and degree completion.

A somewhat similar initiative is found in south central Pennsylvania thanks to the Manufacturing Association of South Central Pennsylvania (York, PA). This manufacturers association sponsors a manufacturing apprenticeship program through its Metal Working Skills Consortium.[2] The local schools also do not provide assistance to the association to offer its related training. Thus, the related training is conducted in house by the consortium itself.

In both these examples, small manufacturing firms were able to solve their mutual issues—inability to locate and hire skilled machinists—by joining together as an association to collaborate in developing an administrative process for registered apprenticeship.

There are several benefits of these collaborative arrangements. Costs are spread among the association membership and undoubtedly kept lower than what any single firm would have experienced alone. Recruitment of candidates for training is accomplished as a group. When an external provider of related education and training was sought, negotiations were done as a single entity with the power of a larger industry and economic development driver.[3]

An additional benefit of firms coming together to do apprenticeship is that if one particular firm does not perform a particular aspect of a given trade, another firm can open its door to afford the apprentice an opportunity to master that aspect of the trade. This thus allows for sharing of capabilities across the partnership. Additionally, the leveraging of financial and facility resources by a group of employers permits the hiring of a staff member (even if only part-time) to oversee the program's operations and apprentice interface.

BUSINESS ADVOCACY GROUPS

Some business and industry advocacy groups also have a potential value in promoting 21st-century American apprenticeship, because these groups offer the following:

- A familiar and comfortable venue for local business to participate in apprenticeship training program delivery and sponsorship;

- A single industry-based skills standard to which apprenticeship training can be focused, directed, and delivered;
- A basis for assessment and evaluation of achievement of these skills, including through issuance and endorsement of a credential attesting to achievement of journeyman status in the industry;
- An opportunity to team with others in the community in delivery of apprenticeships;
- The economic value of group participation in a community-based project.

In the automobile retail sales industry, the Washington Area New Automobile Dealers Association (WANADA) has long been a leader and advocate for automotive service technicians.[4] It has sponsored a technician apprenticeship training program to provide its National Capitol area member dealers with technicians dating back to the mid-1970s. I was its first apprenticeship program coordinator and related education instructor (working through a local community college). WANADA has created a separate 501(c)3 foundation, the Automobile Dealer Education Institute (ADEI), which is the administrative organization for registered apprenticeship. ADEI has a board of directors consisting of member dealers and allied firms. ADEI employs a staff member to interface with apprentice, dealer, and related training organizations. Apprenticeship-related training is provided through several educational venues, including public school adult education in Northern Virginia and Montgomery College (MD) continuing education.[5] ADEI offers scholarships to cover the costs of related instruction program tuition to students who are interested in becoming apprentices. [6] Again, the leveraging of an industry association for its individual members provides a venue to acquire apprenticeship support services as a group, rather than firm by firm.

CONSORTIA

Another configuration of industry collaboration that is growing in popularity is the consortium. In this arrangement, firms representing a wider array of industries share their collective resources to operate a program to meet their needs for apprentice training. These firms also bring a community college and area high schools into the fold. In North Carolina, a movement called Apprenticeship 2000 was initiated by two firms, Daetwyler USA and BLUM USA, both of whom were finding it difficult to hire technically competent service technicians for their mechanical production equipment. These Charlotte region firms eventually were joined by six other firms, mostly headquartered in Europe, that were familiar and comfortable with the process of apprenticeship. The consortia met with Central Piedmont Community College and collaborated to form Apprenticeship 2000 to offer qualified and selected apprentices a four-year apprenticeship, paid college tuition toward an associate's degree in mechatronics engineering technology (credit also accruing from OJT), paid benefits, and a guaranteed job after completing the apprenticeship with an earned degree.[7]

Box 6.1

Apprenticeship—North Carolina Style

North Carolina is witnessing a growing number of regional partnerships for registered apprenticeship in collaboration with its community colleges. Young workers are increasingly able to dual-enroll in registered apprenticeship and a community college program leading to an associate's degree. This is happening as a result of a number of European small employers who relocated to the state and brought their cultural workforce development solutions with them—not unlike what was witnessed at the founding of our nation.

The genesis of this development dates back to around 1990, when Daetwyler USA, a Swiss-based firm, moved into the state from Long Island to manufacture "Doctor Blades," a specialty consumable product in the rotogravure printing process. As the firm expanded, it began having difficulty locating service technicians to support the business. Nearby, BLUM USA, another firm with an Austrian heritage, was having a similar problem locating skilled talent. The two firms began a collaboration that eventually led to a consortium of eight firms agreeing on a mutual solution—registered apprenticeship, called Apprenticeship 2000. Recognizing that none of the firms could alone develop a program similar to what they all experienced in their home countries, they agreed to do so cooperatively.

A partnership was developed with Charlotte-area high schools to recruit youth who had a sincere interest in technical subjects and who were interested in a career in mechanical or electrical technology. The firms designed a four-year registered apprenticeship similar to those used by their Swiss and Austrian home office firms. Participating firms include BLUM USA, Chiron, Daetwyler USA, Pfass, Sarstedt, Siemens, and Timken and have indicated that their motivation is to ensure a continuous supply of skilled talent to be able to replace retiring technicians and maintain company growth. Firms have also indicated that the ultimate cost to provide a four-year apprenticeship inclusive of salaries and college tuition is about $160,000. Graduate apprentices can expect a guaranteed job and starting salary of about $44,000 plus benefits.

Apprenticeship 2000 served as a model and catalyst for two other North Carolina consortia, one called the North Carolina Triangle Apprenticeship Program (NCTAP). This program has as its community college partner the Wake Technical College. The other, Apprenticeship Catawba, comprises several firms partnering with local high schools and Catawba Valley Community College.

Statewide structures to promote and market apprenticeship and, in some cases, to support business use of apprenticeship are also emerging. In Michigan, at Governor Snyder's initiation, the Michigan Economic Development Corporation (MEDC) led the creation of MAT2—Michigan Advanced Technology Training, an apprenticeship approach to business training based on the German model. The MEDC provides the clearinghouse for reaching youth apprentices in high school and matches them with preregistered participating firms. The MEDC also works with area community colleges to develop degree programs to complement the technology areas slated for apprenticeship.[8]

South Carolina's state business leadership took a somewhat similar approach by providing funding and a structure to locate registered apprenticeship consultation and support to business inside of the state's technical college system. A staff of six regional apprenticeship consultants now reach into business to support recruitment and registration of firm and apprentice and aid in the firm's identification of related education services through the colleges.[9]

JOINT APPRENTICESHIP TRAINING COMMITTEES

Perhaps the original collaborative organization for delivery of apprenticeship in the United States, the Joint Apprenticeship Training Committee (JATC), is another venue for bringing firms and employers together in the interest of apprenticeship training. The JATC has its roots in the Fitzgerald Act, which created a national system of apprenticeship in the United States. This committee's purpose is to create a means for employers to come into dialogue and to plan programs in combination with workers' representatives, then interfacing with government apprenticeship administration.

Joint apprenticeship training committee structures offer potential value in promoting 21st-century American apprenticeship, with these committees offering the following:

- A structure suitable for interfacing of state/federal departments of labor, businesses, business groups, labor, apprentices, and community colleges;

- A central organization through which to register apprentices and endorse standards and issue completion cards/certificates;
- A structure to advocate for business use of apprenticeship.

Although fewer than 20 percent of registered apprentices are now unionized, the JATC is still a viable concept. The JATC can be the venue to fund the program; set standards; recruit, interview, select, and evaluate apprentices; and arrange for related training and education. I found some rather unique and creative approaches taken by firms and colleges to work together through the JATC.

In Indiana, organized labor and employers and the state community college have joined together for apprenticeship training, recognizing that their mutual interests can best be served by that collaboration. The genesis of this labor–higher education partnership dates back to the mid-1990s. IVY Tech Community College suggested that the "joining together of higher education and the technical training expertise of the JATC provides the apprentice with an opportunity to enjoy the educational strengths of both the college and JATC."[10] A registered apprentice dual enrolling in one of a number of Indiana's listed JATC apprenticeships and an IVY Tech community college will receive the journeyman card from the Indiana Department of Labor and an AAS degree from IVY Tech upon completion of the registered apprenticeship and specified courses at the college. IVY Tech has an additional partnership with the National Labor College (NLC) to transfer its AAS in apprenticeship technology into NLC's four-year degree.

Ohio's Jerry Sue Thornton, president emeritus of Cuyahoga Community College (Ohio), cites a similar JATC partnership arrangement made by Tri-C and seventeen of the northeast Ohio labor organizations for trades-related training and dual enrollment pathways for nineteen specialized disciplines. She described these arrangements as a process for achieving regional economic development through these win–win arrangements.[11]

In the early 1990s, the College of Southern Nevada (CSN) established partnerships with southern Nevada's organized labor JATCs "to meet the growing need for a properly trained, highly skilled, and educated workforce."[12] CSN actually has an entire academic division devoted to serving the registered apprenticeship community. The college provides an opportunity for registered apprentices in several building trades unions to take general education courses and apply OJT to technical course credits toward completion of an AAS degree.

At the national level, probably the best-known JATC is the National Joint Apprenticeship and Training Committee for the Electrical Industry (now known as the Electrical Training Alliance), comprising both the National Electrical Contractors Associations (NECA) and the International Brotherhood of Electrical Workers (IBEW). As I mentioned in an earlier chapter, the IBEW's Local #3 set the standard for a marriage of registered apprenticeship and a community college degree. Local #3's successes have influenced the National JATC for the Electrical Industry to promote this partnership as well. The programs, nationwide, through local JAC's affiliated with the IBEW, have had their programs reviewed by the American Council on Education (ACENet), and they have articulated an agreement with Pellissippi State Technical College toward an AAS degree.[13] The National JATC also sponsors a summer National Training Institute for apprenticeship instructor training.

Another public service profession example is the California Fire Fighter Joint Apprenticeship Committee (CFFJAC), which is cosponsored by the Office of the California State Fire Marshal, representing management; and the California Professional Firefighters, AFL–CIO, representing labor. As they state, "[w]hen fire departments and their respective labor associations subscribe to the CFFJAC, they are agreeing to provide their apprentices valuable instruction while meeting the CFFJAC standards, which parallel the State Board of Fire Services and the National Fire Protection Association standards."[14] CFFJAC has approximately 151 California fire departments as members and around 6,000 registered apprentices. Each fire department has a local JAC created for local coordination. The statewide JAC also provides the venue for statewide recruitment and physical agility testing prerequisite to admission to a basic fire academy (CPAT). CFFJAC also provides support to member fire departments with additional training beyond the basic firefighter standards. It works with other state and national organizations to develop and deliver homeland security training topics, wild land fire training, and other skill areas as needed.

The California Fire Fighter Joint Apprenticeship Committee is a member of the California Apprenticeship Coordinating Association. This statewide coordinating body is the uniform advocating body for registered apprenticeship throughout California.[15] This organization also coordinates with California's workforce innovation boards to link registered apprenticeship opportunities with WIA funding.

WORKFORCE INNOVATION BOARDS

Last, another form of community-based organization unique to the United States is the workforce innovation board. Workforce innovation boards (WIB) came into existence as a result of the legislation the U.S. Congress created to flow monies into the states and communities for approved forms of workforce training—such as registered apprenticeship—now through the Workforce Innovation and Opportunity Act of 2014 (WIOA). The legislation specified the composition of membership of a WIB, including representatives of local educational institutions and community colleges. I sat as an executive board member of The WorkPlace, the workforce investment board of southwestern Connecticut, while serving as a dean of workforce programs for Norwalk Community College. The new (2014) Workforce Innovation and Opportunity Act replaced the former Workforce Investment Act. However, the WIB is still the local funding mechanism for these monies.

Workforce innovation boards have a real value in promoting 21st-century American apprenticeship for businesses. WIOA places emphasis on funding on-the-job training such as apprenticeship and collaborations of local organizations for training. WIOA favors all aspects of apprenticeship and accordingly will be in an ideal position to provide firms and consortia of businesses:

• Access to a wide diversity of potential workers as apprentices;
• Access to funding, including Workforce Innovation and Opportunity Act and other private funds or grants appropriate for related expenditures in apprenticeship training;
• Promotion and recruitment of apprentices for business across the entire community or region;
• Access to worker/trainee supports including day care, counseling, transportation, etc.

WIBs also have an ability to attract additional monies in the forms of federal and state and private workforce development grants and gifts from local citizens and businesses. WIBs are uniquely situated within a community and can be very effective partners for local businesses. Community colleges are statutory members of these boards. Under the new legislation, many more WIBs will prioritize support for registered apprenticeship.

For example, I found that the Gloucester County (NJ) Workforce Innovation Board has been involved for some time in promoting on-the-job training through apprenticeship. Structurally, it created an Apprenticeship and Workforce Development Committee that oversees opportunities to bring together WIB clients in need of workforce training with firms that are willing to or use apprenticeship to train their workers. Their webpage lists various WIB partners who administer the several apprenticeable trades in their area. They also work with their Youth Council to promote youth apprenticeship opportunities.[16] Apprentices can enroll in Gloucester County College and matriculate toward an AAS in Career Technical Studies and apply 25 credits earned as part of their apprenticeship toward the degree.

I also noted that as part of California's Strategic Workforce Development Plan 2013–2017, the California Secretary of Labor, Workforce and Development Agency issued a letter to California WIBs regarding their state-registered apprenticeship program. The letter underscored the value of apprenticeship to growing California's worker skills and talent base. It called to the attention of the WIBs the fact that of the 55,000 apprentices currently registered (at the time of the letter), 22,000 were in nonconstruction occupations, including firefighters, safety officers, and light rail system workers, among others.[17] Similarly, in South Carolina, with the expansion of registered apprenticeship at the insistence of business and the South Carolina Chamber of Commerce, the State Workforce Innovation Board included the expansion of registered apprenticeship within its incentive structure for local WIB regions.[18]

With the new WIOA in place, workforce innovation boards can fill a void for an organization strategically located regionally throughout the United States with the staffing and funding to promote registered apprenticeship from high school to adulthood. The structure is in place, and all the key community members, from community college to business to organized labor, are WIB members. Now, key funding is available for registered apprenticeship program operation and expansion—and this is mandated in the act.

COMMUNITY-BASED ORGANIZATIONS

Community-based organizations can also provide a venue for partnerships of business, educational organizations, and registered apprenticeship. One such organization is Communities in Schools, which sponsors the Philadelphia Urban Technology Project. Underwritten by a grant from the funding provided by the U.S. Department of Labor to facilitate registered apprenticeship in high-technology, high-demand occupations, the Philadelphia School District is offering youth a two-year Computer Support Specialist Registered Apprenticeship Program.[19]

A BRIDGE-BUILDING ORGANIZATION

During my research, I have come across a very unique partnership initiative that I want to highlight. NJ PLACE—New Jersey Pathways Leading

Apprentices to a College Education—came into existence as a result of recognition, by a multitude of New Jersey–based educational organizations, labor unions, and government agencies, of the need to both promote apprenticeship as a training process and provide apprentices a pathway to higher education. The ability of this partnership to work is based on additional partners—those organizations that exist to equate or build bridges between higher education and workplace learning or training. The process is based on a review by (1) the American Council on Education's College Credit Recommendation Service, (2) the National Program on Noncollegiate Sponsored Instruction (PONSI), or (3) Thomas Edison State College's review of the training design schedule, with the registered apprenticeship agreement stipulating how much college credit, and at what collegiate-level credit, should be awarded. New Jersey's community colleges agree to accept the stipulated apprenticeship training toward a designated AAS degree. NJ PLACE is administered by the NJ State Employment and Training Commission. The process is one of its kind from my research, but funding ceased on January 1, 2014—hopefully to be re-established at some point. The articulation agreements are expected to be continued.[20]

POLICY RECOMMENDATIONS

Based on my review of successful partnerships of business for registered apprenticeship, I offer the following as recommendations to foster more such partnerships in the interest of increased use of apprenticeship training.

- Workforce innovation boards are in an excellent strategic position to promote business use of registered apprenticeship. WIBs can refer apprentice worker candidates to firms and provide funding to help the firm and apprentice to undertake training. WIBs can also introduce firms to each other to form consortia that can aid firms to share resources and capabilities. Community college leaders can position their colleges to be catalysts for these activities, the community college being a mandated member of the WIB.
- Industry and trade associations should consider promoting apprenticeship as a training methodology within their spheres of influence and among their member firms.
- Firms and industry associations should consider the virtues and benefits of forming joint apprenticeship training committees to centralize resources and capabilities for registered apprenticeship training. This

can include applying for funding and grants; sharing expenses for training; recruitment, screening, and selection of candidates; and the like.

- Regional and state economic development organizations should consider how they can promote registered apprenticeship across their areas of responsibility. Similarly to Michigan's success story, this may include catalyzing programs locally, serving as a central point to bring together firms and training candidates, attracting statewide grants from the federal government, promoting two-year degrees, and so forth.

7

The Community College: An American Innovation at the Center of the Partnership

Our nation has been very fortunate over the past century to be served by a truly unique higher education institution—the American community college. Starting with Joliet Junior College in 1920, this institution came into existence to provide quality, low-cost, easily accessible, post-secondary education to those who could not afford the more "elite" university. This community college invention would provide the following:

- General college courses equivalent to the first two years of a university program—initially termed university-parallel or college-parallel courses. These were the general courses (freshman English, college algebra, general social sciences, physical sciences, etc.);
- Workplace preparation through career and technical subjects in occupational areas identified as needed by the community served by the college;
- Adult and continuing education offerings needed or desired by the local community. These might include general high school diploma preparation, industry certification preparation, or other subjects desired by local citizens.

The concept of a local and universally accessible college caught on quickly, and the movement spread across the nation in just a few decades. By the mid-1950s, virtually every state in the nation had a system of local community colleges. Many of them started as a branch of the local high school and then broke away.

Today's community college provides transferable associate's degrees that meet regional accreditation requirements for transferability to a university toward a bachelor's degree. These community colleges also provide associate's degrees in career and technical studies. However, even these degrees are becoming more recognized for transfer as the movement toward ensuring career ladder higher education is becoming more popular.

However, the focus of this writing is on the community college as a partner in delivery of registered apprenticeships. Most international apprenticeship training models have a system in place for the apprentice to attend a school for related technical or vocational studies. In Germany, this is called the "Berufsschule" (vocational school for vocational education and training, or VET). The Swiss use a similar system of partnering with VET schools to complement the on-the-job training portion of the apprenticeship. Allow me to propose that we look at the U.S. community college as the community-based institution that is in the best position to not only be a partner, but also serve as a catalyst for expansion of registered apprenticeship by being the training method of choice for workforce and career development.

Why?

Let's look at the potential that the community college offers to firms or industries desiring to expand their workforces or simply to fill vacancies through apprenticeship:

• First of all, the community college occupies a pivotal position in the community.

The community college is chartered as a local institution with an elected or appointed board of trustees drawn from local or regional citizens and residents. No other institution serves as many diverse constituencies with academic, career and technical and avocational courses and programs, counseling, testing and assessment, and, in many cases, medical services. My college provided degree accruing courses, testing and assessment, noncredit general interest courses, recreational activities, a dental clinic, day care services, a culinary program restaurant, cosmetology services, and a year-round after-school and summer youth program.

Thanks to its board of trustees, the locally based leadership is well connected into the community and usually well respected by business and civic leadership. In turn, the community college leadership can help promote and support business with the services necessary to make apprenticeship function well. However, that leadership must recognize the economic development benefits accruing to the community and local business base and to the apprentice as a student, as well as to the college in terms of enrollment potential.[1] All this was demonstrated at Cuyahoga Community College when its president established a partnership with the local construction trades industry to support apprenticeship training.[2]

Next,

- The community college already has interorganizational relationships and partnerships in place with all or nearly all necessary partners for apprenticeship program operation.

Community colleges already work with community-based organizations such as chambers of commerce, industry associations, workforce investment boards, the Veterans Administration, state departments of labor, and the like. In some cases, these organizations have staff offices residing on the college campus. Serving as a programmatic catalyst with these partners for apprenticeship training with local businesses is a natural next step. Bringing together students as apprenticeship candidates with local and regional businesses, the department of labor, the VA, and so forth is a natural progression. Again, the college academic staff needs to recognize the mutual benefits brought to academic and workforce programs and to students, as well as the economic development benefits brought to the community by building a stronger bridge to industry through serving as a catalyst for registered apprenticeship. North Carolina's Central Piedmont Community College has proven that point through its partnership with Apprenticeship 2000.

Community college career advisory committees.

Additionally, community colleges will have in place active career advisory committees made of up local businesspeople to oversee each career and technical program, including their curricula and standards. This is a program's essential link between education and industry. Career advisory committees may fill some of the role of the professional association in the Swiss system or the industry union in the German model. UK apprenticeship uses a system of industry sector councils. U.S. community college career advisory committees are a statutory necessity under the Carl D. Perkins Technology Education Act if a school or college is to be able to use Perkins monies in its programming. The act discusses committee composition and meeting frequency. Care must be taken to ensure that the program advisory committee members represent all aspects of the occupation and include both worker incumbents and supervisors.[3]

Registered apprenticeship programs also have an oversight committee requirement pursuant to the Fitzgerald Act. I suggest that, when a firm's apprenticeship program partners with a community college for educational support, a co-membership arrangement be made wherein one or several members are members of both committees, thus ensuring effective communications between both organizations.

Community colleges can provide more services to apprenticeships than just the required related classroom training.

* The community college has the resources to provide student recruitment through wide community outreach to identify students who might benefit from apprenticeship training.

A valuable service to a firm or business is recruitment of students as apprentices. The community college reaches deep into the community and can provide this service to the employer. Through its normal outreach protocols, including secondary schools, religious and community-based organizations, news media, and the like, the college will be in a position to ensure effective student-as-apprenticeship recruitment and meet employment regulations that firms must follow.

Community colleges have a structure and system in place for ongoing student recruitment. They do this through their relationships with local high school districts, faith-based organizations, community-based organizations, etc. The community college staff knows how to reach all citizens in the community. No other higher education organization reaches the depth of diversity that the community college does. This is what employers want and need in recruiting potential apprentices, as expressed by 51 percent of firms responding to a U.S. Department of Labor, Employment, and Training (DOLETA) survey of apprenticeship sponsors.[4]

Additionally, as a result of the existing partnerships of the secondary schools and many community colleges under the 21st-century American youth apprenticeship program, established high school and college partnerships for youth apprenticeship will benefit employers, linking existing proven young workers with continuing apprenticeship opportunities. The Swiss, in particular, demonstrate the importance of reaching youth while in high school with career awareness information and the opportunity to begin career training earlier through apprenticeship (similar in some aspects to our youth apprenticeship).

* The college has the resources in place for student testing and assessment to determine academic readiness to be an apprentice.

Apprenticeship programs generally have entrance requirements for basic aptitude and achievement testing.[5] The community college already has in place protocols for assessing potential students for readiness to tackle college work. The college assesses an incoming student's skills in both reading and computational skills to ensure that the student is up to the standard necessary for college-level work. Many colleges use ACCUPLACER© testing online for immediate results.[6] This information is also available for the employer and, through the partnership with the college, will be in place for entry-level work as an apprentice. The college testing center staff and capabilities can be helpful to the employer during the ongoing apprenticeship program. As the apprentice advances from year to year and the firm seeks to do an assessment of apprentice progress (cognitive and/or performance) the testing center staff can help develop the protocol or merely use what the firm has in place.

Community colleges also have the ability to set up and operate assessment centers for specialized assessments, such as physical agility testing, including the Candidate Physical Agility Test (CPAT).[7] We conducted this type of assessment for both fire and police academy recruitments.[8]

- The community college can provide dual-enrollment services to the student—admissions as a college student and registration assistance as an apprentice with the state department of labor.

Some community colleges also have apprenticeship coordinators on staff to aid the apprenticeship registration process through the department of labor. They also have staff expertise in place to do the testing and assessment and screening to assist employers in matching apprentices to entry requirements. Dual enrollment of registered apprentice and community college degree or certificate provides a career ladder as well as a lifelong learning opportunity (see Figure 7.1).

- The community college can rapidly respond with the necessary programming to support a wide range of apprenticeship training areas.

Community colleges provide academic and workforce education services, along with community education services desired and needed by citizens, residents, and businesses. Developing the necessary courses and specialized training is a service the community college has mastered. The college's academic leadership should understand that supporting apprenticeship will have a positive effect on the college's workforce programs and ensure a higher education career ladder for the college student as an apprentice.

Figure 7.1

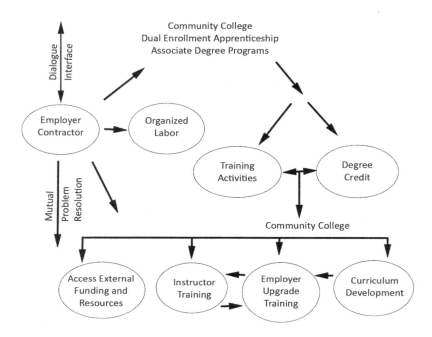

The community college typically specializes in adult education learning experiences. Our American community colleges have special capabilities for working with business and industry to design customized educational programs. A U.S. Department of Labor, Employment, and Training Administration (DOLETA) survey indicated that 41 percent of employers/sponsors surveyed indicated a desire for help finding good-quality related instruction.[9] The composite of all of these experiences is an ability to design and develop and administer apprenticeship programs.

The college is also able to provide academic services:

• Coursework that meets the requirements as the related training component of the apprenticeship;

• Courses in subjects, including math and English, that might be needed to bring the student to the level required to take college courses in the general education subjects required to matriculate toward an associate's degree;

- Associate's degree or certificate-level courses supporting apprenticeship subject major;
- Recognition of apprenticeship on-the-job training as college credit toward selected degrees and certificates.

Prior learning assessment (PLA)

Some newly hired apprentices will have prior work or college experience. Under 21st-century registered apprenticeship federal policies, apprentices can request PLA and advanced standing in the apprenticeship. Community college administrators must recognize that today's student does not want to have to repeat academic work already mastered and accomplished. This includes on-the-job training and legitimate life experiences. The community college has in place an assessment protocol to review this prior learning or prior work through Prior Learning Assessment (PLA) with the American Council on Education (ACE).[10] The college can then recommend to the employer any advanced standing that is appropriate or post to the student's transcript appropriate advanced standing toward the degree or certificate. This has now become an essential component of registered apprenticeship in demand by both apprentices and employers.

Similarly, the community college can assist the employer in assessing prior performance skills mastery if the firm is considering an applicant's prior work performance for advanced standing in the apprenticeship. Many colleges have arrangements with the National Occupational Competency Testing Institute (NOCTI) for such performance assessments against industry competency standards.[11] NOCTI can also be helpful in designing a competency-based apprenticeship program standard.

To make this happen, the college's academic leadership should recognize the legitimacy of structured and competency-based on-the-job training through apprenticeship for college credit toward appropriate degrees and certificates. Apprenticeship OJT is rigorous and challenging. An apprentice should have an opportunity to benefit from dual enrollment and a higher education credential ladder. The mechanisms are in place—it's a matter of attitude and desire on the part of the college. I can attest that once this door is open, enrollments, including full-time enrollments (FTEs), will demonstrate the ultimate value to the partnership.

- The community college also brings supplemental funding for a student's education to the partnership.

Apprenticeship-related education and training in other nations is supported by either the employer or the government. U.S. business is beginning to recognize this as an essential motivating component of the apprenticeship arrangement for the student. Seventy percent of DOLETA-surveyed firms/sponsors indicated that they paid for apprentice-related instruction, and 23 percent of the apprentices paid for their instruction. The college is able to access several forms of supplemental funding that a typical business would not be able to identify alone, bringing significant cost savings for employers:

- U.S. Department of Education—Pell Grant funds to pay for college tuition.
- U.S. Department of Education—Carl D. Perkins Technology Education Act funding to support the technical courses in the apprenticeship program. This might include equipment, tools, and materials for on-campus lab courses.
- U.S. Veterans Administration funds to eligible veterans as apprentices.
- Workforce Innovation and Training Act funds to offset apprenticeship training costs. The community college is a mandatory partner on the local WIB board, and apprenticeship is now a preferred workforce training process.
- State tuition specialized assistance.
- Funding to support a program coordinator for the apprenticeship program.
- Private grant funds for scholarships and program development.
- Special populations funding via government partners to supplement funding such as vocational rehabilitation and veterans benefits.

All these resources and capabilities are exactly what the 21st-century American apprenticeship calls for and are why the community college partnership has been cited as an essential component of this movement's ultimate success.

BARRIERS TO THE COMMUNITY COLLEGE

So why isn't the community college partnering and participating in apprenticeship program delivery in a bigger way?

- Lack of good information across the entire community college about what apprenticeship is all about.

Community college leadership and staff should become more familiar with the process of registered apprenticeship and why the community college has a "golden opportunity" to be at the center of this business partnership. Additionally, employers need more information on how the community college can be of assistance, as expressed by 55 percent of those surveyed. The current structures for promoting registered apprenticeship are via the U.S. Department of Labor's or state department of labor's offices of apprenticeship. Generally speaking, these organizations have not overtly reached out to community colleges with apprenticeship information. The Obama administration has initiated a voluntary Community College 21st-Century Apprenticeship Consortium to provide a mechanism to disseminate best practices and assistance to the colleges and business community. At the state level, the New Jersey department of labor had supported apprentices by building articulation agreements with New Jersey community colleges for pre-assessed courses and on-the-job training and pre-negotiated credit agreements for registered apprenticeship programs. Funding for this unique project ended in January 2014.

- Senior community college leadership's view of apprenticeship as an ancient and outdated instructional modality.

Unfortunately, too many college presidents and chief academic officers see apprenticeship as a historical method of training with absolutely no relevance to modern-day higher education or even technical education. For many years, as I wrote and spoke about the virtues of formal and registered apprenticeship and community college support for apprenticeship, I appeared to be among few academics in higher education administration doing so. CEOs of community colleges need to recognize the need to partner with business and industry to deliver the best technical education possible. No longer can the college go it alone—that has been made impossible by costs of sophisticated equipment, capped enrollments in many high-tech programs, lack of qualified instructors willing to work for college salaries, low enrollment demands for some programs, and many other issues all mandating partnering for training.
    Next,

- A misguided belief that registered apprenticeship is the training process owned by organized labor.

Though apprenticeship has been used heavily by organized labor, labor programs are not in the majority any longer. Only approximately 20 percent of registered apprentices nationwide are associated with organized labor employment. In a number of instances, labor has reached out to the community college for related instruction programs. More will be discussed about these particular programs.

- The apprentice's needs for college academic skills remediation.

Another barrier is one created by the apprentice. The apprentice does not have a strong desire to earn a college credential, which might be brought on by a history of poor academic performance. The apprentice's academic skills (basic reading and math in particular) cause him or her to partake in remediation before taking college-level courses. In my experience as a program coordinator for a fire science program and as a college administrator, this was the single issue holding back our students from achieving the degree or certificate.

All community colleges have a means to assess and deliver appropriate remedial or developmental education courses. The apprentice must be directed to partake of these courses. The employer must provide the motivation to the apprentice to take the remediation, requiring the apprentice to complete the degree or certificate as part of the apprenticeship agreement. Fees are generally able to be covered through WIOA funding or similar funding.

A review of the current practices across America's community colleges reveals that many are partnering with apprenticeship providers to provide related classroom training in an adult education or noncredit venue. From my perspective, this is short-sighted: Those colleges are missing out on an opportunity to glean academic full-time equivalent funding. Doing so limits the apprentice's ability to progress academically toward an eventual degree. Competency-based program standards provide the baseline for validating apprenticeship-related instruction as college degree or certificate creditworthy.

- Lack of understanding of registered apprenticeships, based on competency-based standards, on the part of college leadership.

College CEOs and academic leaderships must understand that community colleges need to ensure that their career and technical program designs are based on competency-based standards produced by industry experts. These become the building blocks upon which dual enrollment of registered apprenticeship and community college degrees or certificates are built. Competency-based standards are also part of 21st-century registered apprenticeship policies. I will add that it is often the use of industry-derived standards that solidifies the partnership between community college and industry itself.

Florida's colleges have compiled a repository of these standards at the state education department level. Termed curriculum frameworks, these standards are prepared by level of career and technical program, including secondary career, adult/vocational, and community college degree or certificate.[12] These standards are developed and periodically validated by business and industry groups to ensure that they remain reflective of the skills, knowledge, attitudes, and abilities of a journeyman-level job incumbent. Care must be taken to ensure that programs are using up-to-date and recently validated industry standards. Earlier in my higher education career, I served in a facilitator role for development of some such standards. I later used these standards to develop and revise career and technician programs at two Florida community colleges. However, these standards are a baseline, requiring that the individual college and its program advisory committee (which I discuss shortly) ensure that it is up to date, reflecting current skills needs.

In another approach to industry standards, Germanna Community College in Virginia, at the request of several local manufacturers sponsoring apprentices, adopted the National Center for Construction Education's (NCCER) Competencies and Objectives for the Industrial Maintenance Mechanic and its associated training modules as a standard for its related education curriculum and in the GCC associate's degree.[13]

Today there are a plethora of industry standards organizations across the various occupations and industries. A firm engaged in apprenticeship training will need to identify the standards that best emulate the skills and knowledge appropriate to that firm's occupations. The firm should be able to turn to the college staff for guidance and assistance with this decision.

- Community college availability of a process and resources for faculty recruitment and training.

Most community colleges have a process for faculty development of their full-time faculty. Some extend this opportunity or requirement to their adjunct faculty. Not too many view their registered apprenticeship staff as adjunct faculty if these people are attached to their continuing education branch. Faculty are the lifeblood of a training program. This statement is as true for programs operating under the roof of the college as for journeymen working for the firm and serving as instructors or mentors to apprentices on the job. Both these roles require skills in teaching and learning. To mitigate concerns that community college faculty lose touch with their occupational disciplines after leaving a firm or an industry, faculty must be continually trained and updated in both the skills of teaching and the particular industry or crafts that they are teaching. Some European countries, such as Portugal and the Netherlands, make specific and rigorous educational, occupational, and training requirements of mentors or journeymen assigned to an apprentice.

For the skills requirements of college instruction, most colleges have professional development and certification programs in place for their entire faculty. However, the challenge for college administrators is finding ways and means of keeping career and technical program faculty up to date in their respective areas of expertise. In my career, I have used several methods, including partnering with local business for (1) faculty externships or semesters back in industry and (2) industry-based training programs.

For example, the International Brotherhood of Electrical Workers and National Electrical Contractors Association sponsor a summer training institute for apprentice instructors, apprenticeship committee members, and program managers.[14] The program brings in master instructors and professional educators to present in their respective areas of expertise to apprenticeship instructors. Florida community colleges have a professional development program for all community college faculty. Apprenticeship providers using a community college can have their journeymen instructors serve as adjunct community college faculty to benefit from these professional development opportunities.

• Inconvenience of college course schedules for employers and apprentices.

Often inflexible course scheduling makes it difficult or impossible for apprentices to attend on-campus courses.[15] Fixes for this can include blended online and in-class instruction, online sections of courses, and, when possible, segregated sections for apprentices, scheduled at the plant or on campus.

• Lack of tailoring of community college courses to apprenticeship needs.

A very prevalent concern, in this age of high-tech specialization, is that it is very possible that nothing in the catalog will work for the related instruction.[16] The fix here is for the college to identify a representative industry association and search its resources for corporate training materials from which courses can be constructed to industry standards. It's a time consuming process, but it's one that has worked for me in meeting industry needs. Germanna Community College staff worked with their several firms and identified industrial maintenance course materials developed by the National Center for Construction Education and Research (NCCER).

AN EXAMPLE OF SOME CURRENT PARTNERSHIPS

At this point, let's take a look at some of the community college–registered apprenticeship arrangements in place around the United States.

Several of North Carolina's community colleges have been increasing their service to local business groups that have been sponsoring registered apprenticeship. Central Piedmont Community College (CPCC) is part of the Apprenticeship 2000 consortium of firms in the Charlotte region. CPCC's role in the partnership has several facets, including participation in a summer institute–pre-apprenticeship course program for high school students that have applied into the apprenticeship and have made it through the first few "layers" of screening and interviews. The summer institute allows the student to gain some experience and familiarity with the manufacturing processes and to demonstrate their abilities to master technical concepts and group work. Based on student performance in this summer experience, students are then identified as potential apprentices and matched to employers to start their apprenticeship, upon high school graduation. CPCC then offers a mechatronics engineering technology associate's degree for registered apprentices who are dual-enrolled at the college along with their apprenticeship. CPCC also recognizes that the ultimate success of registered apprenticeship rests with the college's counseling staff's appreciating the apprenticeship process and the offering of occupations available to the students. Accordingly, the college participates in a counselor orientation process inside the firm to educate staff.

Additionally, CPCC offers general registered apprenticeship assistance to its business community. CPCC advertises: "Let CPCC help your company set up an apprenticeship program. With this as a part of your training strategy, you can rely on the College to deliver:

- Support for determining the candidate intake process.
- Coordination of NC Department of Commerce activities and agreement process.
- Detailed information on the requirements and elective course work available with certificates, diploma or degree requirements.
- Convenient sponsorship option to CPCC (payment process)."

Central Piedmont Community College provides a comprehensive slate of apprenticeship program support services to handhold a small firm through the process of beginning and maintaining an apprenticeship training program.[17]

Box 7.1

Central Piedmont Community College

Apprenticeship Program Support

"Set Up an Apprenticeship Program"

What to Expect
The scenario below is a typical sequence when establishing an apprenticeship program.

Meeting One: We learn about your unique objectives and operations. We also introduce our team and share details about the apprenticeship program, the potential advantages to employers, offer case studies and student examples. Often, this happens onsite at your company and includes a tour for CPCC faculty and/or a workplace counselor.

Meeting Two: We invite you to our campus and lab facilities, where you may interact with students and faculty. In this meeting, we discuss how our learning objectives and student skills can be applied in your workplace.

Meeting Three: If we've determined a good fit, the third meeting will be to plan the details of the implementation. We'll go over guidelines and expectations so that we can best evaluate the experience.

Source: Central Piedmont Community College, "CPCC Consultation Meetings with Prospective Employer on Registered Apprenticeship," https://www .cpcc.edu/clc/workplace-learning/apprenticeship-charlotte-resources.

The Apprenticeship 2000 program provided a model for North Carolina business. The word spread, and two other consortia developed. One of these is Apprenticeship Catawba, which includes several firms, including Saratedt, Technibilt, Tenowo Nonwovens, and ZF Friedrichshafen AG, working with two local school districts and Catawba Valley Community College. This consortium requires that student applicants have an average high school GPA of 3.0 and recommendations from the guidance counselor/technical subjects instructors. CVCC recruits students with the tag "Enjoy a career working with robots, computer aided design or electronics?"[18] The third consortium, located in the Raleigh–Durham triangle area, "NCTAP— North Carolina Triangle Apprenticeship Program," operates similarly and in partnership with Wake Technical College.

South Carolina has also attracted much attention nationally with its statewide initiative centered in the South Carolina Technical College System (SCTCS). The environment is right for registered apprenticeship, as European companies form the largest segment of employers in the state, especially German firms. It was these firms, collectively, that requested the SCTCS's help expanding their services to registered apprenticeship. Apprenticeship Carolina, a division of the SCTCS, was begun in 2007 to provide increased visibility to the community, consultation to firms seeking to use apprenticeship as a training process, recruitment of students as apprentices, and education of the public as to the tax credits and other benefits to using apprenticeship. The action to fund SCTCS and to create this new service was driven by a 2003 report by the South Carolina Chamber of Commerce citing the low participation rate of South Carolina employers in registered apprenticeship. The Chamber of Commerce then approached the president of SCTCS to enlist assistance turning this around. This newly created SCTCS division was eventually staffed with full-time business outreach representatives throughout the state.[19]

Two Washington state community colleges, Bates Technical College in Tacoma and South Seattle Community College, have business and industry partnerships for apprenticeship program delivery. Bates Technical College cites affiliations with eleven state-approved apprenticeship programs. It posts program coordinators for these programs on its website.[20] For the most part, these are in the traditional manufacturing and construction trades. Bates Technical College also offers its students, as apprentices, the opportunity to earn an Apprenticeship Studies Degree (AA-S) by presenting 6,000 hours of apprenticeship on-the-job training and 432 hours of apprenticeship-related education (earned via the employer), as well as 20 credit hours of Bates Technical College general education courses in residence at the college. These college courses are in communications/English, math, and social sciences.

South Seattle Community College (SSCC) provides more-detailed information on its website about the role of an apprentice and career opportunities after graduation to journeyman.[21] The site is tailored to prospective apprentices and prospective employers contemplating hiring apprentices. The site has a link to the Washington Department of Labor and Industries and its registration system. SSCC has approximately eighteen business and industry partners listed on its site as cooperating programs with the college. Again, these are in traditional manufacturing and construction trades as well as in the aerospace industry, which offers some more high-tech applied technology occupations. SSCC offers similar opportunities to earn a nontransferable AAS degree in Multi-Occupational Trades, wherein the apprentice must present 6,000 of apprenticeship on-the-job training certified as completed, plus 450 clock hours of related education taken through the employer and certified as such, plus completion of 15 credits of SSCC college credit courses in applied composition, technical writing, applied math for technicians, psychology of human relations, and project management.

Wisconsin has a long history of recognizing apprenticeship as a process for mastering a trade or occupation and secure gainful employment. As previously discussed, Wisconsin's labor statutes were the first to address the process of apprenticeship. Wisconsin also has a highly nationally recognized system of two-year technical colleges—sixteen of them throughout the state. Northcentral Technical College (NCTC) in Wausau, as one of these colleges, has partnership arrangements with area employers and employer groups. On its webpage, NCTC provides an easy to read and understandable description of the apprenticeship learning process, the indenturing agreement, and the several partners' roles and responsibilities. It directs the apprentice candidate to the application process. For each trade (e.g., electrical and instrumentation) there is a linked college webpage that details the trade work, physical and educational requirements to apply into the apprenticeship, the terms of apprenticeship, and the application procedures. The process here requires that the apprentice candidate locate an employer and apply to the department of labor via the employer. NCTC offers the apprentice and employer related instruction classes taken one day a week for eight hours. It also offers the apprentice remedial or enrichment math and reading courses through its learning center.

Again, a significant number of productive and sizeable firms have apprenticeship in their heritage. For many years, the Newport News Shipbuilding Company has operated a multicraft apprenticeship training school employing more than 800 apprentices, with about 250 new hires annually. The company has negotiated with two Virginia community colleges in the Hampton Rhodes area, Tidewater Community College and Thomas Nelson Community College, for college courses to complement on-the-job training with related education and training and afford the apprentice an opportunity to earn a college degree along with career training. The company has also developed an academic partnership with Old Dominion University for apprentice coursework in the engineering field toward a bachelor's degree—one of the first of its kind for apprentices.[22]

Unique in a number of ways, Empire State College of the State University of New York has numerous business and industry, government, military, and organized labor partnerships. The one I view as its flagship partnership is an associate's degree apprenticeship partnership with the International Brotherhood of Electrical Workers and its New York City Local #3. Local #3 sets as a specific requirement in its apprenticeship agreement the earning of the associate's degree. And in this partnership, the apprentice's having completed the associate's degree in labor studies and having completed the apprenticeship training may now, as a journeyman, continue on to the Bachelor's Degree in Labor Studies at Empire State College. This partnership provides for a true career ladder education for the electrician seeking additional educational opportunities. This relationship exemplifies the 21st-century American apprenticeship that the government is promoting.

Other employers and employer associations have taken the lead from IBEW Local #3. The United Association Local #1, Plumbers and Pipefitters Apprenticeship program also accrues 40 college credits for completion of its apprenticeship training to the associate's degree in labor studies at Empire State College.

PROGRAM EVALUATION

In all registered apprenticeships, apprentices are evaluated on their on-the-job progress semi-annually and annually to review their overall progress as well as for salary advancement purposes. Their related coursework is evaluated after each course completion. The college will evaluate those courses that it offers to the apprentice. It will evaluate their on-the-job training if that experience carries a course number for administrative purposes. If it is presented by the apprentice for PLA credit, then the college will follow the procedure already outlined.

Program evaluation for 21st-century American apprenticeship can be done by the college in partnership with the employer and other partners. This is called formative evaluation, being used primarily for program improvement purposes.

POLICY RECOMMENDATIONS

I suggest that the community college is the natural catalytic partner for 21st-century apprenticeship:

The community college can support local businesses in numerous ways, as already discussed, not least through recognition of registered apprenticeship as workforce training that can culminate in an associate's degree.

My suggestions for policy consideration for community college support and participation with registered apprenticeship are as follows:

National/Macro Level

- The American Association of Community Colleges and the League for Innovation in the Community College should be encouraged to take the lead in advocating for the U.S. community college to provide the related education and training component of the U.S. registered apprenticeship.

As in most all of the European and other worldwide formal apprenticeships, we need a focused and dedicated institution, nationwide, that understands and accommodates registered apprenticeship. National community college advocacy organizations such as the American Association for Community Colleges and League for Innovation in the Community College should officially promote registered apprenticeship as a preferred method of workforce education among the nation's community and technical colleges. The community college should provide academic programming that accommodates the firm's educational and training needs and schedule. The culmination of the apprenticeship must also include the apprentice's earning of an associate's degree.

Institutional Level

- Community college leaders should also recognize the responsibility of the college to support a firm or business with the administrative aspects of registered apprenticeship. Such assistance may include helping them register their apprenticeship program with the department of labor, recruiting potential apprentices and testing and assessing those candidates, developing related instruction and evaluation, and co-enrolling the apprentice toward an associate's degree or certificate.

Partnerships

- Community college leaders should work with area secondary schools and business to develop youth or pre-apprenticeship programs that segue into adult registered apprenticeship and community college degree matriculation.
- Community college leaders should foster partnerships with their local workforce boards to promote registered apprenticeship opportunities for all segments of the community.

Academic Programming

- Community college leadership and faculty should build internal articulations of noncredit apprenticeship-related instruction and college credit degree programs.

- Community colleges should recognize industry certifications earned by apprentices as creditworthy for college coursework.

- The community college can wrap apprenticeship on-the-job training and related education around an associate's degree to create a higher education career ladder for the apprentice.

- Statewide clearinghouses such as New Jersey's NJ PLACE are excellent venues for cataloging and promoting articulated and agreed-upon apprenticeship program college credit equivalencies. Perhaps community college leaderships and department of labor officials can agree to develop these clearinghouses across the states.

- Community college leadership and faculty should recognize registered apprenticeship by developing associate's degree programs to accommodate these programs.

- Community college faculty should recognize national industry standards as baselines for registered apprenticeship on-the-job training and related instruction.

- More national standards projects similar to the NMTA standards and the IBEW/NCEA electrical worker standards need to be undertaken. I suggest something resembling the Canadian Red Seal Program for the United States. Perhaps the most important undertaking for the United States to ensure a national system of registered apprenticeship is to design and develop a system of uniform national standards for apprenticeship.

- Community college faculty should help businesses develop their in-house apprenticeship instructors and on-the-job mentors and aid in instructional technologies, including distance learning.

- The IBEW/NECA national apprenticeship program provides training and professional development for instructors annually, in a summer institute. European apprenticeship programs require training of their apprenticeship instructors. The United States also needs to recognize the importance of professional development for apprenticeship instructors.

Thus the American community college is a natural catalytic partner for America's 21st-century apprenticeship.

8

Skills Standards and Industry Credentials: The Framework for Apprenticeship Training and Pathway to College Degrees, Diplomas, and Certificates

WHAT'S ALL THE FUSS ABOUT?

When I met with business owners and operators and discussed their views on sponsoring apprenticeships, I quickly discovered that details relating to worker skills standards were not of much interest or part of employers' personal expertise. Perhaps one of the greatest barriers perceived by a businessperson when considering sponsoring apprenticeship is that of having to specify training standards to the department of labor and supporting educational providers in sponsorship agreements. However, apprenticeship training should be predicated upon defined industry standards for an occupation, trade, or profession, and as such, is an important preplanning consideration.

In my research for this book, I found little attention given to defined industry standards in American registered apprenticeship, in general, and not just from business operators. I know that the employer defines what an apprentice is to master in the way of job skills and related training, but I can't really discern how, or where in the process, that is happening. However, there are exceptions to this finding. An IBEW apprenticeship is very well defined and documented. When apprenticeship is used in a small firm for customized or specialized occupations, based on the firm's own design, such an apprenticeship is less defined. At this point in the U.S. registered apprenticeship milieu, industry-recognized and industry-endorsed standards are not routinely being used in the course of apprenticeship training. Ayres (2014) underscores my concerns that too many employers cannot discern what an apprentice knows or has mastered as a result of an apprenticeship today owing to inconsistent and ill-defined standards from employer to employer and state to state.[1]

Firm owners are not necessarily expert in all facets of all of the jobs performed at the company. Owners want to be able to hire competent workers, especially highly trained technicians, and are having trouble doing this. Even so, knowing the standards and work processes for a given occupation is essential to conducting a quality apprenticeship training program. How to decide what to train? Methods are available for an employer to use to acquire these worker skills standards, but what we do not have in our U.S. apprenticeship structure or practices is an "intermediate" industry-sponsored system of worker skills identification and competency certification to support both employer and apprentice. In this chapter, I discuss some other countries' practices when apprenticeship is more in the mainstream of workforce development.

THE BASICS OF SKILLS STANDARDS AND INDUSTRY CERTIFICATIONS

A little history. Here in the United States, standards for industry training became a discussion topic during the 1970s when prominent American industries, such as the automotive manufacturing and servicing and electronics industries, were caught broadside by high-quality products made in Japan. The U.S. responses soon became known as Total Quality Management (TQM) and focused upon an entire company or firm's production process, including personnel training.

The worker skills standards movement became more prominent over the last two decades of the 20th century and into the 21st century, leading up to the information technology boom, at which point IT firms found it difficult to identify trained people to staff the various aspects of that growing industry. Few formal IT training programs existed, and schools and colleges, along with industry training itself, had little to go on in developing courses and programs. A need existed for industry standards for use in judging, comparing, assessing, and developing worker competency.

WHAT SHOULD BUSINESSPEOPLE AND POLICYMAKERS KNOW ABOUT WORK SKILLS STANDARDS?

Work skills standards.   A standard is a baseline on which a judgment or act is predicated. In the workplace, a worker performance or skills standard is the benchmark to which a job must be performed. Such specifications identify the composite knowledge, skills, and abilities (KSAs) that an individual must possess to be deemed competent in an occupation in the workplace. These composite KSAs must be measurable if they are to be useful. In apprenticeship parlance, the standards for job performance are termed work processes. These describe the job performance requirements that constitute a job or occupation for which the apprentice is training—more simply put, the procedural and technical rules generally followed by members of an industry.

The National Workforce Center for Emerging Technologies (2003) developed a skills standards "pyramid" that precisely presents the logical development of occupational skills standards. Evans (2002) describes a worker skills pyramid as three-tiered: The first tier is a set of foundation and employability skills—knowledge and abilities required of all workers in that field and universal in nature (e.g., problem solving, teamwork). The second tier is sets of technical skills, including knowledge and abilities common to all workers in that industry cluster. The third tier is the specific technical skills for a particular occupational job classification.[2] Table 8.1 shows the pyramid of competencies.[3]

Skills standards provide a framework for developing apprenticeship training programs, developing outcomes measures for training, and providing a systematic means for measuring ultimate employee competence. Skills standards also help align employee skills with industry certifications. Skills standards help the worker achieve stackable skills certifications and are portable regardless of advancement and job changes.

At the national level, at the turn of the century, federal legislation created the Goals 2000 Project. As a result of the Goals 2000: Educate America Act, the National Skills Standards Board was established to create a national system of voluntary skills standards.[4] Industry by industry, groups of knowledgeable workers and employers were to come together to analyze jobs and occupations and establish these benchmarks.[5] What was these benchmarks' intent?

Table 8.1   Three Skills Tiers

Tier III Industry-Specific Technical Skills Knowledge and abilities unique to individual industries or organizations	Examples include • Knowing and complying with (1) company practices and organization protocols; (2) industry legal requirements; and (3) company and product standards • Understanding and effectively using industry terminology
Tier II Technical Skills, Knowledge, and Abilities Skills common to all jobs within a career cluster across all industries	Examples include • Proficiently using software and hardware tools • Proficiently using Internet techniques • Understanding hardware/system architecture • Troubleshooting software and hardware problems
Tier I The Set of Foundational Skills (SCANS) Knowledge, abilities, and personal qualities required of all workers for them to be successful in today's workplace	Foundational Skills • Basic skills (reading, writing, arithmetic) • Thinking skills • Personal qualities Workplace competencies • Time and resource management • Interpersonal skills • Information use and management • Systems understanding and management • Technology use

Adapted from *Building a Foundation for Tomorrow's Skills Standards for Information Technology,* National Workforce Center for Emerging Technologies (Bellevue, WA), 2003, p. 3.

Skills standards should form the basis for apprenticeship program curriculum design. Apprenticeship program administrators should use these standards to create programs that are state-of-the-art. Certification exams, administered *independently* from a college, can then be benchmarks of apprenticeship program success in delivering contemporary content when apprentices take these exams after completing college courses and programs. Employers take note. For apprentices, taking college courses as apprenticeship-related instruction, these industry certifications can also serve as benchmarks for on-the-job (OJT) instruction.

However, setting and maintaining worker skills standards must be a continuous process—both within individual firms and across the entire industry. As industry grows and changes, associated worker skills standards also morph. These changes must be reflected in training of the worker through retraining courses taken periodically and enforced through the requirements for recertification tests for various worker certifications. The Goals 2000 Project was not widely accepted across business and industry—being, after all, created by government, not by industry.

The National Skills Standards Project has, to a limited extent, helped bring these various constituent groups together toward the common goal of worker and industry excellence. As the digital age has created new forms of work, the game content production industry has needed formal definition. In Washington state, this work represents a major industry, with many firms needing talented workforces. The industry and Lake Washington Technical College came together to produce the first National Skills Standard for electronic game production technicians.[6] Industry representatives locally based and nationwide provided the input to this project. As Jacoby (2013) stated: "Who better than employers to set standards? Not only do companies know exactly what skills they need in the workplace; they're also far more likely than educators to be aware of how those skills are changing and how 'occupational' training should change to keep up."[7]

INDUSTRY REACTIONS TO IDENTIFYING WORKER SKILLS STANDARDS BASELINES

Some industry or trade organizations set up and establish worker skills standards for occupations within an industry. Industry members representing their particular firms and the specialty under consideration provide the input and guidance to construct the set of work skills standards. As I have indicated, there are numerous industry-based organizations representing nearly all industry sectors, some repositories for their industry's worker standards. Some of these include the National Center for Construction Education and Research (NCCER) in the construction trades industries, the National Institute for Metalworking Skills (NIMS) in the machining and metal working industries, and the National Workforce

Center for Emerging Technologies in information technology. There is no coordination of these organizations' efforts for the purposes of registered apprenticeship.

The National Center for Construction Education and Research (NCCER) began as a group of 125 industry representatives and firm CEOs looking for a non–government-regulated (thus oftentimes unregistered) means of producing trades and crafts workers with the skills to do the various construction jobs: "Our vision is to be universally recognized by industry and government as the training, assessment, certification and career development standard for construction and maintenance craft professionals."[8]

NCCER has identified worker skills standards in seventy craft areas. They have developed curricula to support training in these areas, along with accompanying assessments leading to stackable NCCER credentials that are then placed into a national registry for the benefit of apprentice, journeyman, employer, and educational institution. The system is designed so that the employer provides the on-the-job training component of the program. Under the revised 2008 federal apprenticeship regulations, recognized industry skills certifications such as NCCER, when earned by the apprentice, can be used to satisfy part of the competency-based apprenticeship requirements. These credentials become "stackable" toward advanced credentials and ultimately lead to journeyman status.

I used NCCER curriculum materials for a construction trades–related training program while at Pensacola Junior College. NCCER provides insights into how an industry or business sector can form for the purposes of identifying worker skills for a trade or occupation and then supporting the same with curricula models, guidance, and assessment and certification. This is as close to the EU model of industry association supporting apprenticeship as I have found in the United States.

Similarly, the National Institute for Metalworking Skills (NIMS) Precision Skill Standards project was formed by the several metalworking trade associations to provide a benchmark for worker competency in the various metalworking and machining occupational areas. Their motivation was a decline in American vocational–technical education worker training capabilities that necessitated industry's stepping up to provide workers with precision manufacturing skills. The National Tooling and Machining Association (NTMA)—NIMS project has developed ANSI-accredited skills standards and competency assessments in twenty-four operational areas. There are fifty-two NIMS skills certifications. [9] And employers can make the decisions: A small group of machine tool shop owners elected to use NIMS industry standards and curriculum materials in their apprenticeship-related instruction courses offered through Germanna Community College (VA) in the Fredericksburg, Virginia, area.

The NTMA has also created the NTMA-U customizable competency-based and self-paced modular support curriculum project to help apprentices prepare for NIMS certifications. These modules have been reviewed by several colleges for credit toward two-year degrees in machine tool manufacturing technology–related majors.

The National Workforce Center for Emerging Technologies has also provided extensive work to identify worker skills standards sets for work in the information technologies professions and occupations. Skills standards include database development, digital media, enterprise systems analysis and integration, networking design, and technical writing. Per the pyramid previously discussed, these standards are articulated in three tiers, ranging from general worker workplace skills to technical skills to industry-specific job skills in specializations.[10]

Public safety is another industry sector that has grown for national and international security reasons over the last decades. In the fire prevention and control industry, the National Fire Protection Association created technical committees to develop standards for use as a basis for certifications in the major industry areas. These include firefighter qualifications, and the Association supported the development of a professional job skills and qualifications certification process, as well as a certification registry, by initiating a National Professional Qualifications System (NPQS). The emergency medical services industry has also developed a National Registry of Emergency Medical Technicians that has set and maintained training standards for these occupations.[11]

A GLIMPSE AT INTERNATIONAL APPROACHES TO WORKER SKILLS STANDARDS DEVELOPMENT

Numerous European nations, as well as Australia and Canada, have systems of apprenticeship trade and industry associations to identify, define, and maintain worker skills standards for occupations in their respective industries. We need such a system for apprenticeship standards administration. Ayers contends, as I do, that we must set as a national goal establishing registered apprenticeship as a credible form of worker certification from an employer's perspective. We need uniform sets of industrywide standards that attest to apprentices' skills, knowledge, and competencies. Furthermore, this will aid higher education, by allowing community colleges to recognize the depth and level of training and education that a registered apprentice has attained, and applying said education and training toward college degrees.

In Great Britain, Wales, and Scotland a system of industry sector skills councils and bodies supports apprenticeship and worker skills standards. The seventeen sector skills councils and five sector skills bodies are independent employer-led organizations responsible for developing high-quality skills standards and defining occupational standards and job competencies to serve as apprenticeship frameworks. Sixteen different and diverse national skills academies subordinate to the sector skills councils link businesses and apprentices to training by maintaining lists of appropriate training providers that can deliver those standards. These councils and bodies then seek to ensure that the correct data and evidence for each qualification is verified before issuance of certificates of completion to apprentices. English industry sectors are quite broad and extensive and may serve as one possible model for U.S. apprenticeship. The skills standards setting and certification process is coordinated by its umbrella organization, the Federation for Industry Sector Skills and Standards.

I note that there are a number of areas represented on this UK sector list that are unique and not widely used by American apprenticeship. Filmmaking and media, health sciences, energy production, sports, and fitness, among other industries, are growing U.S. industries and can benefit from use of apprenticeship to grow and develop a workforce.

Britain's prime minister, David Cameron, touted apprenticeship as a 21st-century workforce training system that puts learners and employers first, setting it out as a modern vision for skills training for the British people worthy of significant funding from the British government.[12]

Switzerland's apprenticeship system operates around *industry-operated sector organizations*. Committees of industry experts meet periodically to review and set occupational standards for their profession. These sector organizations, such as the Center for Young Professionals in the banking industry, provide a focal and coordinating point for industry training of young apprentices. In the case of banking, a young person receives industry orientation and some technical training, funded by the Swiss banking industry. In the school component, 16- to 19-year-olds generally study languages, mathematics, history, ethics, and law, with an individual bank providing the on-the-job training.

I believe that Canada's Interprovincial Standards Red Seal Program for apprenticeship standards holds much promise for the United States. Canada also uses a system of industry sector councils to set worker standards for apprenticeship to ensure a supply of trained and competent workers for Canadian businesses. In addition to standards setting for the

Box 8.1

UK Industry Sector Skills Councils and Bodies and National Skills Academies

- The Building Futures Group – (facilities management; housing; property, cleaning and parking)
- Financial Skills Partnership – (accounting; finance; financial services)
- Skills for Care and Development – (social care; children; early years and young people's workforces in the UK)
- Cogent Skills for Science Industries – (chemicals; pharmaceuticals; biotechnology; life sciences; health care; bio-medical; environmental technologies; nuclear; oil and gas; petroleum and polymer)
- Institute of the Motor Industry – (retail motor industry)
- Creative Skillset – (television; film; radio; interactive media; animation; computer games; facilities; photo imaging; publishing; advertising; fashion and textiles)
- Construction – (building trades)
- Improve Food and Drink – (manufacturing and processing and associated supply chains)
- Skills for Health – (entire health sector)
- Creative and Cultural Skills – (craft; cultural heritage; design; literature; music; performing; visual arts)
- LANTRA – (land management and production; animal health and welfare; environment)
- Skills and Justice – (community justice; court services; custodial care; fire and rescue; forensic science; policing and law enforcement; prosecution services)
- Tech Partnership Skills for the Digital Economy – (software, Internet and Web, and IT services; telecommunications and business services)
- People 1st – (hospitality; leisure; passenger transport; travel and tourism)
- Skills Active – (freight logistics; wholesale industry)
- Energy and Utility Skills – (gas; power; waste management; water)
- Science; Engineering; and Manufacturing Technologies – (aerospace; automotive; composites; electrical/electronics; marine; metals; mechanical; space)

Sector Skills Bodies:

- Skills CFA – (business administration; human relations; industrial relations; customer service)
- Skills for Security – (private security industry)
- Engineering Construction Industry Training Board
- Pro Skills – (printing; mineral extraction and processing; health, safety, process, and manufacturing of furniture, glass, ceramics, coatings, and paper)
- Summit Skills – (building services engineering)

National Skill Academies

- National Skills Academy for Construction
- National Skills Academy – Creative & Cultural
- National Skills Academy for Enterprise
- National Skills Academy for Health
- National Skills Academy for Financial Services
- National Skills Academy for Nuclear
- National Skills Academy for Food and Drink
- National Skills Academy for Power
- National Skills Academy for Social Care
- National Skills Academy for Materials, Production and Supply
- National Skills Academy for Process Industries
- National Skills Academy for Retail
- National Skills Academy Railway Industries
- National Skills Academy IT
- National Skills Academy for Sports and Active Leisure
- National Skills Academy for Hospitality

Source: Federation for Industry Sector Skills and Standards, http://fisss.org/sector-skills-council-body/directory-of-sscs/.

fifty-five skilled trades, Canada's industry sector councils perform the following tasks:

- Develop industrywide human resource plans;
- Create national training programs;
- Establish occupational standards;
- Nurture a training culture;
- Inform young workers of the changes and opportunities in particular industries;
- Attract young workers to specific industries;
- Address a wide range of issues related to technological change, quality standards, planning, and human resource development;
- Provide a cooperative effort, a strategic alliance of all the players in the Canadian labor market—individuals, company owners, corporate leaders, labor, government, and educators.[13]

What is it about Red Seal that makes it useful and doable for America?

- It is designed to be administered and used on a provincial level, so it can work at the state level.
- It provides for a national standard of excellence for each recognized trade.
- Each trade represented was analyzed through an occupational analysis process that produced a set of standards representative of trade practices nationally.
- An examination is developed to support final apprentice evaluation for each trade, based on the national occupational standards.
- The structure of analysis consists of blocks of skills: tasks, subtasks, and key competencies, plus required knowledge, safety, tools, and equipment—all elements necessary to provide details of the trade.
- Potential student information about the trade, job opportunities, working conditions, and job prospects across the nation are all included for counseling and decision making.
- Registered apprenticeships are developed solely on this standard for Red Seal occupations.

I believe this to be a very good model for consideration across the United States.

INDUSTRY WORKER COMPETENCY CERTIFICATIONS— THE NEW CREDENTIALS

When we examine the requirements for obtaining work in most industries that are in demand in this second decade of the 21st century, we find that many, if not all of them require a worker to possess or obtain an industry-issued or -endorsed skills certification. These certifications are designed to measure, assess, and document that a worker has attained and mastered all the requisite skill set. Some apprenticeable occupations are built on stacks of industry certification. As I wrote in my League for Innovation Leadership Abstract in 2002, "certification is a confirmation of one's adequate knowledge and skills in a specified occupation or occupational specialty."[14]

Industry certifications are predicated on worker skills standards, so industry certification and registered apprenticeship go hand in hand. Having achieved the requisite skills and knowledge through registered apprenticeship, an apprentice graduating to journeyman will undoubtedly be able to test and qualify for associated professional certifications. And in many cases, this is exactly what we see.

For employers, industry certifications become a measure of worker quality control. Industry certifications are often issued for fixed periods of time and require that the holder retest for recertification. Thus these endorsements ensure that journeyman technicians stay current in their fields. Likewise, employers benefit by having the latest technology know-how on staff, something they are happy to advertise.

What are some of the industry standards–based certifications sought after by workers? A review of the information technology milieu reveals the following:

- Microsoft Certified Solutions Associate (MCSA)
- Project Management Professional (PMP)
- Certified Information Systems Security Professional (CISSP)

Jacoby (2013) cites the National Association of Manufacturers (NAM) as aggressively moving forward to endorse selected industry certifications, including NCCER and other like trade groups for NAM members.[15] For example, NAM supported the development of a Manufacturing Skills Certification System together with fifteen certification sponsors. This system provides the baseline for industry training standards and assessments. Thus, if this movement continues across America and in its various industries, the industry credential will become the "sheepskin" of the future. Structured industry training vis-à-vis apprenticeship will be the best route toward that credential. Jacoby says—and I wholeheartedly agree—"curriculum and standards will help spark the creation of [more meaningful] programs."

FROM CERTIFICATION TO COLLEGE DEGREE: THE BRIDGE BEGINS HERE

Employers should be advised that skills certifications have become as much recognized as college degrees in many employment venues, and perhaps even more so in some. Apprentices must recognize that the key to career security is continuing education. It is the worker who must take ownership for continuing education, but employers should recognize that their investment in a worker's education will pay off for the business bottom line as well. A more trained and educated worker is a valuable business asset, as many of our European counterparts attest. And such workers will become more loyal to their employers.

One important first step is to maximize educational opportunity. Employers must advocate the equivalency of selected industry certifications to college credit as they procure related training for their apprentice. With apprenticeship training becoming recognized as equivalent to certain levels of college credit, apprentices should get that credit included on a college transcript as it is earned. Skill certifications can be complementary to college programs and can be an effective bridge to industry.

Most of the prominent professional and technical industry certifications have been reviewed by The American Council on Education (ACE) College Credit Recommendation Service. ACE is a professional association aiming to provide a medium for corporate and adult education organizations, the military, and other specialized organizations to interface with higher education. ACE reviews and evaluates corporate and government training delivered on the job and, in turn, provides a recommendation of college credit amount and level for credit awards toward an appropriate degree by colleges and universities. ACE also provides guidelines for assessing and evaluating on-the-job work experience and lifelong learning experience for college credit equivalency. Accordingly, a student matriculating toward a degree who has earned a recognized certification appropriate to that degree, upon proof of the certification, may receive such college credit. As I remarked in my League for Innovation piece previously cited, this provision by an organization such as ACE provides a lifelong learning bridge from the world of work to the academy.[16]

Other organizations, such as higher education institutions specializing in the adult learner, also have units that perform assessments of professional training and credentials for college credit equivalencies. These include

Thomas Edison State College in New Jersey[17] and Charter Oak State College in Connecticut.[18] Indeed, I have served as a reviewer for Charter Oak State College. When satisfaction cannot be gained from the local community college or vocational trade school, other alternatives exist to provide apprentices access to higher education.

As previously mentioned, in New Jersey, the State Employment and Training Commission developed a bridge service called NJ PLACE.[19] NJ PLACE Degree Pathways has negotiated agreements with the New Jersey community colleges and several public four-year colleges to recognize certifications, credentials, apprenticeship training, and other industry training that have been ACE-reviewed or reviewed by the other higher education review services for college degree credit. An apprentice can receive up to 25 college credits from an eligible apprenticeship program toward an associate's degree in applied science in technical studies at a New Jersey community college. The Leadership in Energy & Environmental Design (LEED) AP building and construction certification is worth five college credits toward a BSAST (Bachelor of Science in Applied Science and Technology) degree in construction at Thomas Edison State College.

In practice, an accreditor organization such as ACE will carefully review a certification's baseline knowledge, skills, and abilities and determine what level of higher education said KSAs would best represent (e.g., LD = lower division or freshman/sophomore; UD = upper division or junior/senior). The evaluator then weighs the breadth of KSAs represented by the certification and judges how many traditional college credits the certification represents. This recommendation is then given to ACE or the sponsoring organization (e.g., Thomas Edison State College, Charter Oak State College).

The college receiving the request for a granting of advanced standing toward a college degree, diploma, or certificate then considers the accreditor's recommendation and reviews it against the coursework requirements for the applicant's degree. In some cases, such as in the case of the NJ PLACE negotiations discussed above, these considerations have already happened as part of prior negotiations.

As I have said and now repeat, "All too often . . . certification is separated, even segregated by curriculum planners. For certification to reach its full potential for work and training, we must partner not only with industry, but with ourselves." Certainly in my experience, such as in the fields of information technology and health, community college programs include preparation of students for certifications appropriate to various offered programs, tracking and analyzing the results for instructional indications including program content. In fact, the current federal Perkins Technology Education Act requires industry certifications achieved by students in programs funded by Perkins as an indicator of program success.

In fact, in the U.S. Department of Labor's newly promulgated 21st-Century Registered Apprenticeship regulations, the provision for an apprentice to be able to gain industry certifications along the process of the multiyear apprenticeship is now codified. Its value as a benchmark of interim accomplishment and skills mastery is recognized by employer/sponsor and worker alike.

All learning has value, and all Americans should be able to accumulate lifelong learning credits toward a higher education. Apprenticeship is a strenuous learning activity, involving significant technical and general knowledge of a particular subject combined with psychomotor skills and related attitudes and abilities. In every respect, it represents as much higher learning as—if not more than—most undergraduate collegiate learning. When combined with the various worker industry certifications that an apprentice can also accrue during the apprenticeship experience, certainly an apprentice ought to have both the opportunity and the encouragement to apply them toward an associate's degree or a higher degree. It's up to us as businesspersons, educators, and policymakers to insist that this becomes recognized and accepted policy.

At the time of writing, the student loan debt outstanding for 2014 is $1.2 trillion. And according to *TIME* magazine in 2014, the average student's college student loan balance is $33,000.[20] Quite a tidy sum all round.

It is thus no surprise to learn that parents and young people are rethinking the smartest path to a good life. And this may not involve a traditional higher education. Let me make one thing very clear: I am not advocating an uneducated American society. I believe strong academic skills are essential, but there are a plethora of paths to that objective.

Employers working with their community colleges considering sponsorship of apprenticeship should consider the following suggestions:

- Identify an appropriate industry group or association and discuss worker skills standards. If that industry group does not have that information, the local community college and the workforce education representative may do the research to identify worker skills standards in the industry cluster;
- Use accepted skills assessments that support worker skills standards to monitor apprentice progress at six-month intervals;
- Consider supporting the apprentice toward earning skills certifications in areas relevant to the apprenticed occupation;

- Consider the value in having an industry association help with the apprenticeship administrative processes, including recruitment, registration, and skills certification;

- Support national policy changes that would create a U.S. version of the Canadian Red Seal apprenticeship standards and accompanying database.

POLICY RECOMMENDATIONS

- A national system of industry worker standards and worker evaluation needs to be established for registered apprenticeship.

This system should be developed much like the Canadian Interprovincial Standards Red Seal Program. It should be capable of marketing registered apprenticeship and providing consumer information about the various trades, occupations, and professions, as well as work opportunities in those fields. This system might interface with state departments of labor to match candidates for apprenticeship with firms seeking apprentices. This system should also be able to provide employers information about hiring apprentices and about available financial incentives.

- National industry standards councils must be established to identify and set worker competency standards for registered apprenticeship and monitor apprenticeships, evaluating program completers and issuing national certifications of competency.

These councils should be similar in composition and operation to the standards councils in Switzerland, Canada, and other countries having well-established systems for apprenticeship.

9

A Model for 21st-Century Apprenticeship Emerges

My several years of research for this book proved very interesting and informative. The confluence of U.S. economic policy and American work-force conditions has provided a backdrop against which registered apprenticeship can prove very useful as a workforce development policy and tool. I envision a model for 21st-century American apprenticeship that focuses the decision making for an employment/training relationship with a firm or business in collaboration with the community college.

At the time of writing, the path taken for career education by America's young people is coming under intense scrutiny. The value of a typical college education is no longer a guarantee. Far too many college students are not attaining jobs commensurate with the costs of a degree or are not completing a degree while still amassing huge debt for an unfinished education. Alternatives to the traditional college education are becoming real considerations, including the other four-year education—registered apprenticeship. As the word spreads through industry groups, chambers of commerce, and other business and civic venues, I hope we in the United States will see the wisdom in returning to registered apprenticeship to continue to grow our workforce talents in the interests of greater national economic development and peaceful prosperity. My model is unique in that it focuses both on the community college as provider of a two-year degree in partnership with employer-provided on-the-job training (satisfying the related education portion of the apprenticeship experience) and on employer support of the overall apprenticeship experience. It calls on the community college to support the employer with student services and business support services to ensure a successful training experience for apprentice and employer alike. The student-as-apprentice experience should begin in high school as a youth apprenticeship and continue with the employer through to the community college degree.

I believe that as the value of employer-directed and employer-delivered training in combination with the last two years of high school and a segue to a two-year and fully transferable college degree becomes increasingly known and recognized, this alternative to traditional American higher education will become increasingly popular, embraced by parents and talented young people alike.

CREATING NATIONAL POLICY REFORM FOR REGISTERED APPRENTICESHIP

We lack a cohesive system for registered apprenticeship in the United States. My model is predicated upon a national policy redesign that includes the following:

- Aggressive marketing of registered apprenticeship to business and industry;
- Aggressive marketing of registered apprenticeship to firms, youth, and parents, emphasizing the benefits of the registered apprenticeship process along with a college degree;
- Regionally based program registration assistance within each state for both businesses and apprentices;
- Creation of a national system of industry skills council to define, develop, and maintain occupational skills databases;
- Development of a journeyman worker certification registry;
- Increased fiscal incentives for firms and apprentices;
- Focused support for registered apprenticeship by the local community college;
- Degree-based related instruction and education;
- Increased use of employer consortia as a support to business;
- Increased business and community organization partnerships for registered apprenticeship;
- Increased use of youth apprenticeship as a segue to adult apprenticeship.

Following is an overview of how 21st-century American apprenticeship is best operationalized.

A REDESIGNED NATIONAL SYSTEM

- A national workforce development policy adopted by both business and education that recognizes registered apprenticeship as a preferred method of workforce training for jobs and professions.

A revisited policy will need to include federal Department of Labor support for employers and apprentices, delivered uniformly at the state level. Rather than a system in which twenty-five states have direct federal support and coordination and the other twenty-five do their own things, we need a single cohesive, uniform system, streamlined to be non-invasive to the employer and apprentice, as a "one-stop shop" operation such as has been created in South Carolina. By locating the apprenticeship consultants in local or community-based organizations, such as a college in the South Carolina Technical College System, all of that state's businesses have their support for apprenticeship close by, available to aid the training process. The South Carolina model has demonstrated that this aspect of the 21st-century model can work for all America, as I discuss further in chapter 10.

From a marketing and outreach perspective, state and local economic development organizations and chambers of commerce should recognize the value of aggressively promoting the value of increased use of apprenticeship training to a state's business community. An example of this was seen in South Carolina when the South Carolina Chamber of Commerce studied the potential outcomes of new apprenticeship policy and moved the legislature to proactive intervention that ultimately increased apprenticeships by several hundred percent in that state. Apprentice candidates will be identified, recruited, tested, and referred to employers by secondary school counselors, community college programs, workforce investment board counselors, and chambers of commerce and local economic development organizations. Again, I discuss more about how this might happen in chapter 10.

- A national registered apprenticeship system redesigned and co-developed by the U.S. Department of Labor, Office of Apprenticeship, and a coalition of industry standards organizations (e.g., National Tooling and Machining Association; International Brotherhood of Electrical Workers; National Association of Manufacturing) that establishes an industry standards council process for all major industry clusters.

Apprenticeship in the United States needs a central portal for information dissemination to all potential stakeholders in the training process, including students (high school and college), out-of-work youth, currently registered apprentices, parents, teachers and counselors, employers and potential employers of apprentices, government officials, and journeymen. The central portal then becomes a repository for information dissemination, which includes:

- Apprenticeship and the process for apprenticing;
- Financial support available to apprentice and employer;
- A national occupational analysis for the job area of interest (e.g., What will I be expected to do and perform in this job?);
- A listing of the jobs, trades, or professions available for apprenticeship;
- Essential general skills necessary for succeeding in the profession or job;
- A listing or registry of employers who have agreed to take on apprentices;
- An up-to-date job bank of available apprenticeship openings;
- Study guides for the national examinations by occupation, job, or profession;
- A guide to how to register for the exams.

Teachers, counselors, and parents will need:

- An educator's guide to registered apprenticeship, as well as perhaps presentations aimed at each of these groups.

My vision of revisited policy includes a framework for industry skills councils that will address national occupational skills development. This is one of the most significant aspects of registered apprenticeship that must be addressed. I strongly suggest that the issue of nationally recognized and industry identified occupational standards can been addressed by using the Canadian Red Seal apprenticeship system model, as well as aspects of Swiss, English, and German systems, to redesign and develop our national system into a true system with uniform industry-developed and industry-monitored worker competency standards. Each industry standards council will be comprised of recognized industry experts. The councils will meet on a regular schedule and will establish linkages and processes for keeping abreast of changes in technology and practice within their industries. They will reflect these changes in the skills standards databases and transmit the changes to the organizations responsible for the competency examinations.

To assess the apprentice's progress and ultimate competence upon program completion,

- A national testing and evaluation organization (e.g., the American Council on Education or College Board) will establish a process for testing and certifying against the industry standards councils' standards. An organization such as the National Occupational Competency Testing Institute (NOCTI) will do likewise for the on-the-job skills portions of an occupation.

These industry-defined worker competency standards will be validated, allowing firms and licensing bodies to universally recognize the validity of the training provided by employers, large and small, across America. To further support worker credentials,

- A national registration repository system will be established that lists apprentice program completers who have passed their national examinations. This registry will also include industry certifications in addition to the journeyman credentials.

Such a repository and registration system works well in a plethora of occupations and industries, including the firefighter and emergency medical services industries, in which national standards and certification have existed for many decades.

FUNDING AND INCENTIVES

As we continue to look at a redesign of our national registered apprenticeship process, employers will be motivated by adoption of fiscal policy that creates:

- A tax credit (state and federal) that offsets reasonable costs of that training for those firms that train their own workers via registered apprenticeship.

As part of the South Carolina initiatives, small business in that state lobbied for and received a package of tax credits that support their registered apprenticeship training process. All state business leaderships will need to undertake such initiatives. Similar in structure to what economists have recommended for such a tax credit program, eligible businesses receive $1,000 per year per apprentice for up to four years. This, coupled with other funding opportunities (Workforce Innovation and Opportunity Act and the S.C. Enterprise Zone Retraining Credit) about which consultants can advise the firm, makes registered apprenticeship appealing. I further advise that consideration be given to adopting a policy that recognizes the value of getting secondary school students (aged 16–18) involved in youth or pre-apprenticeship as a segue to adult apprenticeship by affording the employer a bonus of an additional $1,000 per youth apprentice employed for more than 20 hours per week. As I will discuss in chapter 10, several states have incentives for employer-sponsored youth apprenticeship.

Next, it would be wonderful if there were an increased level of social responsibility among businesses in the United States that motivates firms with the capacity to train workers in excess of their present workforce needs for smaller or less capable firms. As in Switzerland, these firms would then receive an additional stipend above the nominal tax credit to offset their costs of such training. Accordingly, I look for adoption of a civic stance by business that is facilitated by:

• State governments that provide subsidies to firms for training apprentices in excess of those firms' current need for workers.

Business involvement in career and occupational education can provide the foundation for an improved system of workforce education across both secondary and community college education. Americans have begun to look around the world at nations that have developed strong national partnerships of business and education to educate and train their youth. In the Swiss system, vocational training happens within the firm that is providing the apprenticeship training. The firm has actual teaching labs and classrooms and a dedicated instructor.

• Firms will take on registered apprentices from both local high schools and community colleges to provide workforce training in a wide cross section of occupations and professions.

The Swiss and other national apprenticeship systems provide career education in a cross section of professions, technical fields, and trades. These include banking and finance, retail occupations, health technology, information technology, law, public safety, entertainment and recreation, and so forth. My model extends to all fields.

A FOCUS ON THE COMMUNITY COLLEGE

Community colleges are uniquely American institutions of post-secondary education that have served local communities by focusing on the first two years of higher education, career education, and workforce training, and service to community and business. They have excelled at their mission. Accordingly, I urge community college leadership to take on the task of supporting employers for registered apprenticeship. This will begin with the college's chief executive officer recognizing the value of registered apprenticeship as a workforce development tool and the responsibility of the college to support the firm in delivering the training and to support the student in recognizing the academic achievement of the apprentice.

The registered apprenticeship process begins in secondary school, where we have a partnership of secondary school, employer, and community college. As was demonstrated in North Carolina consortia, the process can work well. Commencing in high school, partnerships of business and community colleges will continue to develop, ultimately leading to:

- Community colleges' adopting a policy of partnership with employers to support registered apprenticeship.

As the attractiveness of registered apprenticeship increases, the number of firms requesting community college support services will also increase, and more colleges will hire staff to provide such services. More colleges will engage in:

- Recruitment of prospective apprentices for local firms;
- Candidate testing and counseling to support firms;
- Developmental education to prepare student candidates for apprenticeship;
- Apprenticeship program registration assistance to the firm;
- On-the-job mentor training for the firm.

Some colleges are also providing:

- A pre-apprenticeship "readiness" program and counseling

for candidates needing more academic skills development or desiring more career awareness education before they decide. I found that some community colleges provide:

- Related training through regular academic college courses

leading to:

- Associate's-level college degrees for apprentices.

Some only offer:

• Non-credit related training to the apprentice.

A few colleges, such as IVY Tech Community College, Central Piedmont Community College, and Empire State College, have developed customized associate's degrees for the apprenticeship community.

Again, the South Carolina Technical College System supports businesses in many of these aspects of apprenticeship training. Colleges such as the College of Southern Nevada and Portland (OR) Community College support selected trades organizations' apprenticeship programs with some of these services.

The next legislative accomplishment should be for:

• Modification of the federal Pell Act regulations to recognize registered apprenticeship as a fundable form of higher education.

We hear very clearly from numerous employers that the benefit of related education through a college degree or certificate is very desirable for both apprentice and employer. It is good to see that in some states (Texas and California), policy has made it possible for related education and training at the community college to be provided to the apprentice at no tuition cost. Ideally, policy in all states will soon recognize that the public investment in related education toward a college degree is returned to the economy multifold.

Some firms that have embraced apprenticeship training (e.g., Buhler Aeroglide, AMERITECH Die & Mold) proudly promote the concept on their websites as a recruitment tool for both apprentices and other firms. Additionally, major firms, government agencies, and organizations have begun to promote registered apprenticeship using webpages of their own as the movement gains momentum.

INCREASING COMMUNITY PARTNERSHIPS

The business community is beginning to accept some responsibility for school reform. As a result, it would be fruitful to see,

• A national movement led by business and industry evolve to set up regional consortia of industries to work with high schools and community colleges to provide registered apprenticeships leading to adult apprenticeship and two-year degrees.

High school counselors and parents need to aggressively support these efforts.

The success of North Carolina in joining business together into regional consortia to create partnerships within the local industry base and with area secondary schools and community colleges demonstrates the success to be derived from such an undertaking, as well as the power of a business group to effect change. The North Carolina story should serve as a national model for like consortia to bridge industry and education for registered apprenticeship commencing at the youth apprenticeship level. Perhaps local chambers of commerce or other civic organizations or business and industry associations can bring businesses together into consortia for sponsoring registered apprenticeship.

Moreover, the 2014 Workforce Innovation and Opportunity Act has "opened new doors" for registered apprenticeship. It also builds a bridge for community economic development through matching people in need of work skills with firms in need of trained workers through apprenticeship. As a result of 2014 federal legislation,

- Our nation's workforce investment boards will now need to be promoting registered apprenticeship to clients in need of career and workforce training. WIBs will also be cooperating with community colleges in greater numbers to provide related training toward college degrees.

In chapter 10, I discuss my desire to move forward to implement my 21st-century American apprenticeship model through changes designed to increase awareness of apprenticeship as a workforce development process and by changing current practice and policy to reflect better practices.

10

Join Me and Get Out and Spread the Word

My goal in writing this book is to enlighten my fellow community college and workforce development leaders about the benefits to America of using registered apprenticeship as the primary means for training and educating our workforce. Whether for small business, larger corporations, or government, registered apprenticeship yields benefits to the employer, the apprentice, the economy, and society as a whole.

I am not alone in recognizing these benefits: In recent years, we have seen several state governors provide increased funding to their state apprenticeship programs (Iowa and Michigan), commission special studies of the economic effects of apprenticeship for the purpose of increasing state support to such programs (Maryland), create statewide initiatives to strengthen school-to-work programs through registered apprenticeship (Michigan), reorganize the state support infrastructure for registered apprenticeship (South Carolina), and reduce burdens on business to engage in registered apprenticeship (North Carolina). At the federal level, we have seen the current administration place millions of dollars into registered apprenticeship to incentivize business to engage in this form of career and vocational training. At the time of writing, a bipartisan bill is in a Congressional committee aiming to create a major funding stream for registered apprenticeship.

My goal in this book was to offer insights into why the process works so well and what it will take to reinvent registered apprenticeship for a 21st-century American economy. I do this after careful consideration of all aspects of the world of career education as I have experienced it from the perspective of a vocational educator and study and by analysis and personal observation of the economic development aspects of workforce education through on-the-job training by business and industry—worldwide.

Chapter 9 discussed the elements of my 21st-century American apprenticeship model. The only remaining issue is how to create such a system for workforce education through registered apprenticeship in the United States. I contend that doing so is a realistic and achievable goal if we all work together.

CREATING DIALOGUE FOR A REDESIGNED NATIONAL SYSTEM FOR REGISTERED APPRENTICESHIP

- A national workforce development policy needs to be adopted by both business and community colleges that recognizes registered apprenticeship as a preferred method of workforce training for jobs and professions.

As I have witnessed in several states, the work begins at the local level. Business leadership must first recognize the benefits accrued to businesses and the local economy by focusing attention on workforce education through registered apprenticeship. In South Carolina, an executive at Roche Company believed that the Swiss apprenticeship system was the key to filling the skilled worker gap that the firm was experiencing. South Carolina business leaders eventually came together and commissioned a study to serve as a framework for the legislation that strengthened their state's registered apprenticeship services, creating increased visibility for apprenticeship for worker training by locating those services in South Carolina's technical colleges.

Similarly, several manufacturing firms in North Carolina turned to registered apprenticeship to fill their needs, forming local consortia and collectively negotiating for related educational services, including college degrees through local community colleges. Additionally, the power of the local consortia working together effected a proposed change in state legislation (pending at the time of writing) to eliminate the annual registration fee imposed by the state department of labor on apprentices.

State initiatives can also work. In a few examples I've found, the state's chief executive saw the wisdom in using registered apprenticeship to strengthen the state's businesses and thus its state economy. Michigan's Rick Snyder feared that Michigan's businesses would be unable to locate sufficient trained talent to grow their firms. Intrigued by what he read about apprenticeship in Germany and what he saw on a trip to Germany, he directed a pilot project through the Michigan Economic Development Corporation to bring young people and skills training together through Michigan apprenticeship. Oakland County,

Michigan, economic development initiatives emphasize registered apprenticeship as a business development tool.[1] Iowa's state legislature increased funding by several million dollars in 2014 for Iowan registered apprenticeship. Maryland commissioned a study in 2013 of the economic development benefits of an increased registered apprenticeship effort in that state. And both South Carolina and New Jersey business leaders have embraced the concept of registered apprenticeship. I look for more state chief executive officers to recognize the economic development gains to promoting registered apprenticeship among the state's businesses and employers.

At the federal level, as I have indicated, the Obama administration has put significant funding and policy behind registered apprenticeship. Two U.S. senators, Cory Booker (D) of New Jersey and Tim Scott (R) of South Carolina, introduced the Leveraging and Energizing of America's Apprenticeship Act in 2014, termed the LEAP Act. In addition to providing a tax credit for new apprentices, this bill puts special emphasis on recruiting young apprentices into the skilled trades. The legislation proposes tax credits of $1,500 for apprentices younger than 25 and $1,000 for apprentices older than 25. This bill has bipartisan support.

Initiatives for registered apprenticeship policy should emanate at the business level, and they can begin in the local community. This registered apprenticeship concept being such a natural one, its attraction is unilateral, and support for it spreads quickly.

Government consultation and support to firms is needed. As said in chapter 9, any new policy will need to include federal department of labor support delivered uniformly at the state level. The modification of the state apprenticeship council and support structure will take both individual state (in the case of the twenty-five state apprenticeship council [SAC] states) and federal action, but it is a dialogue worth having for consistency's sake. If each state could place apprenticeship consultants into local community colleges, businesses and prospective apprentices would be well served at reduced cost to the public sector. I'll talk more about advocating for a national policy for community college support of business and registered apprenticeship later in this chapter.

A system of uniform industry-derived standards is needed. The national registered apprenticeship system needs to include provisions for a uniform system of industry-derived standards that are administered by industry and government. The Department of Labor, Office of Apprenticeship, and a coalition of industry standards organizations (e.g., National Tooling and Machining Association, International Brotherhood of Electrical Workers, National Association of Manufacturing) should establish an industry standards council process for all major industry clusters.

A new national policy will need to include a framework for the creation of industry standards councils that will oversee national occupational skills development. As I've said, this is one of the most significant aspects of registered apprenticeship that needs addressing. Again, as I stated earlier, I strongly suggest that the issue of nationally recognized and industry identified occupational standards can be addressed by using the Canadian Red Seal apprenticeship system model as well as aspects of Swiss, English, and German systems to redesign and develop our national system into a true system with uniform industry developed and monitored worker competency standards. Each industry standards council must be comprised of recognized industry experts drawn from a cross section of firms, large and small, within that industry cluster. The industry standards council would be charged to create a list of occupational worker skills, knowledge, and abilities marking a journeyman in a particular occupation, accompanied by the measurable standards of performance for each skill set. To assess the apprentice's progress and competence, the industry skills council would also oversee the production and administration of the examination process for an apprentice upon completion of a program.

A process for testing and certifying against the industry standards councils' standards must be developed. Industry-defined worker competency standards must be tested and validated, allowing firms and licensing bodies to universally recognize the validity of training provided by employers, large and small, across America. I suggest that an organization such as the Council for Adult and Experiential Learning (CAEL) be recruited and requested to guide such a process. CAEL has devoted its four decades of existence to aligning learning and work[2] and thus is perfect for a leadership role in a movement for revitalization and reform of registered apprenticeship in America. CAEL has provided a venue for educators, employers, policymakers, political leaders, and students to engage in meaningful dialogue about lifelong learning opportunities, prior learning assessment for college credit purposes, and workforce education that has had a positive effect on college and university acceptance of workforce learning accomplishments and public policy. CAEL's Learning Counts initiative has created a process for translating prior learning into college degrees through appropriate credit. Perhaps CAEL would take a primary leadership role for the national redesign of registered apprenticeship? I think CAEL is an appropriate organization to take a lead in directing a redesign of our national registered apprenticeship framework—specifically, skills standards databases and apprentice skills assessments and credentials repositories. From these credentials repositories, apprenticeship prior learning can then be bridged to college degree credits.[3] The National Occupational

Competency Testing Institute does the same for the on-the-job skills portions of an occupation.[4]

A national registry for journeyperson workers is also needed. To support worker credentials, a national registration repository system must be established that lists apprentice program completers who have passed their national examinations. This registry can also include industry certifications in addition to the journeyman credentials.

Such a repository and registration system works well in a plethora of occupations and industries, including the firefighting and emergency medical services industries, which have used national standards and certification for years. I believe that firms and organizations currently using registered apprenticeship will also support this policy recommendation. I further suggest that organizations such as those just cited recognize the need for national industry standards and would support, and perhaps wish to participate in, such a national movement. Perhaps the Council for Adult and Experiential Learning (CAEL) would consider leading the creation of such a national registry?

The challenge to our federal Office of Apprenticeship and to the U.S. Congress is to support such national reform. Again, the push for this impetus must come from business leaders nationwide, across the widest possible industry span.

FUNDING AND INCENTIVES

- A tax credit (state and federal) is needed that offsets reasonable costs of training for firms that train their own workers via registered apprenticeship.

As I pointed out in chapter 9, many states do offer a tax credit offset to firms that engage in employee training through registered apprenticeship. Certainly as the movement swells, more states will offer their business communities similar tax credits. Such tax credits popularly center on youth apprenticeship or apprentices younger than age 25. Some states also focus credits on training in industries that contribute to the kinds of economic growth that a particular state wishes to see.

- Related education and training through the community college must be provided to apprentices at no tuition cost.

Policy in all states needs to recognize that the public investment in related education toward a college degree is returned to the economy multifold.

Perhaps one of the most significant social investments a state can make is in providing tuition-free related education toward two-year degrees for apprentices through local community colleges. In addition to the tax credit bill, I also suggest that the U.S. Department of Education's Pell funding be extended to registered apprentices. This would take Congressional action, and it calls for businesses, as well as potential apprentices and parents, to lobby local congressional members to call for such action.

State and federal governments should provide subsidies to firms that train in excess of the employees they need. As I visited Swiss business and became familiar with that country's apprenticeship training structure, what most impressed me was the social conscience of employers. The concept of providing opportunities for career and vocational training of youth, above and beyond what the particular firm required for its workforce, overwhelmed me. How wonderful it would be for U.S. business to take on part of the responsibility for career and vocational education of our nation's youth. Maybe we can incentivize such behavior through state and federal subsidies for employer-sponsored workforce education.

A tax credit structure is needed at the federal level. Hopefully the Booker–Scott legislation will prevail and thus offer more firms the incentive to join in the movement toward employee training via registered apprenticeship. I would also like to point out that with the 2014 passage of the new Workforce Innovation and Opportunity Act, many more apprentices and firms will be able to benefit from the vouchers that can be used by qualified apprentices for registered apprenticeship. Perhaps the National Association of Workforce Boards (NAWB) can take the lead in getting national acceptance by state and local workforce investment boards to aggressively promote registered apprenticeship as a training and workforce development tool to move their clients into gainful employment. [5]

A FOCUS ON THE COMMUNITY COLLEGE

- Community colleges must adopt a policy of partnership with business for delivering programs of career and vocational education via registered apprenticeship.

What would it take for the local community college to support registered apprenticeship? The list of elements for policy design that I offered in chapter 9 includes those services that a community college can provide to a firm or business:

- Aggressive marketing of registered apprenticeship to business and industry through the college;

- Employers, youth, and parents need to be more enlightened to the benefits of the registered apprenticeship process;
- Regionally based program registration assistance within each state to business and apprentice via the college to the department of labor;
- Focusing the support for registered apprenticeship by the college;
- Degree-based related instruction and education;
- Support for development of apprenticeship consortia for the business;
- Support for increased business and community organization partnerships for registered apprenticeship;
- Support for youth apprenticeship at the high school as a segue to adult apprenticeship.

As a former director and dean for business and industry services, I think that feasible. The challenge will be in establishing a national model for the American community college. This will involve the college's chief executive officer's recognizing the value of registered apprenticeship as a workforce development and training tool delivered in partnership with a firm, as well as an accepted instructional methodology for academic credit toward degrees. The South Carolina success story came about because statewide business lobbied for a single state agency to undertake the registered apprenticeship leadership. In those other states having a state system of two-year or technical colleges, that process may be replicable: Alabama, Delaware, Louisiana, Kansas, Maine, New Hampshire, Virginia, Washington, and Wisconsin. Other states having either independent local boards or state coordinating boards will need to sell the concept across their colleges. Perhaps a series of national demonstration grants under a funding mechanism similar to the past Trade Adjustment Assistance Community College and Career Training initiative would be appropriate? Perhaps an advocacy organization such as the American Association of Community Colleges would adopt a position to lobby for the community college to assume a focal leadership role for registered apprenticeship? Or maybe the League for Innovation in the Community Colleges would see the wisdom in this institution's central position to provide business support to registered apprenticeship and take the lead to rally colleges around this role? At the time of writing, the U.S. Department of Labor's Office of Apprenticeship and the AACC have been attempting to attract community colleges to registered apprenticeship through their national registration to be part of a consortium but have met with very limited success. Accordingly, a more aggressive undertaking is needed to bring the colleges along to meet this challenge.

INCREASING COMMUNITY PARTNERSHIPS

• A national movement led by business and industry, evolved to set up regional consortia of industries to work with high schools and community colleges to provide registered apprenticeships leading to adult apprenticeship and two-year degrees, is needed. High school counselors and parents need to support aggressively these efforts.

As I have pointed out in chapter 9 and elsewhere, North Carolina has demonstrated the effectiveness of local consortia of businesses and education (as well as the department of labor) for registered apprenticeship. I suggest that chambers of commerce and local and state economic development entities explore ways and means for creating more such consortia. The return on investment, in terms of parent education, local board of education awareness, school counselor education, and bringing in additional business, can be substantial.

GETTING THE WORD OUT TO AMERICA

Throughout this book, I discuss aspects of community college workforce education and registered apprenticeship about which I am passionate. Are we prepared as American citizens and entrepreneurs to address a shortage of more than 8 million workers having prerequisite levels of education and training to staff our firms and drive our economy? I have long recognized that registered apprenticeship provides both employers and potential workers the best form of occupational preparation for existing jobs under actual working conditions. Moreover, it provides the worker both a paid job and training, contributing useful services to the employer while simultaneously boosting the local economy. When the employer partners with a local secondary school and community college for support and related education toward an associate's degree, on-the-job training further helps the educational institution deliver quality educational programs. What I see here is a win all around for the community. Help me get this message out to our community partners—and thank you for considering my 21st-century American apprenticeship model.

Notes

PREFACE

1. Fuller, Allison, and Lorna Unwin. "What's the Point of Adult Apprentice-ships?" *Adult Learning* (spring 2012): 8–14.

2. Cantor, Jeffrey A. *Cooperative Apprenticeships: A School-to-Work Handbook*. Lancaster, PA: Technomic Publishing Co., 1997.

CHAPTER 1

1. U.S. Department of Labor, Office of Apprenticeship. www.doleta.gov/oa/apprentices_new.cfm#apprenticeships.

2. Fuller, Allison, and Lorna Unwin. "What's the Point of Adult Apprentice-ships?" *Adult Learning* (spring 2012): 8–14.

3. International Labour Organization. "Towards a Model Apprenticeship Framework: A Comparative Analysis of National Apprenticeship Systems." Geneva: 2013. www.ilo.org/wcmsp5/groups/public/---asia/---ro-bangkok/---sro-new_delhi/documents/publication/wcms_234728.pdf. This study, a joint collaboration by the ILO and the World Bank, reviews international experience in apprenticeships and identifies good practices based on cross-country analysis. The report includes case studies on eleven countries' apprenticeship systems—Australia, Canada, Egypt, England, France, Germany, India, Indonesia, South Africa, Turkey, and the United States. It also discusses a framework for a model apprenticeship system.

4. Fuller, Allison, and Lorna Unwin. "The Great Skills Debate." Training-Journal.com (August, 2012): 12–14. www.trainingjournal.com.

5. Journal Report, R1: "The CEOs' Top Priorities." *Wall Street Journal* (December 9, 2014).

6. Holzer, Harry J., and Robert I. Lerman. "The Future of Middle-Skill Jobs." *CCF Brief #41* (2009). Washington, DC: Brookings Institution.

7. Olinsky, Ben, and Sarah Ayres. "Training for Success: A Policy to Expand Apprenticeships in the United States." Washington, DC: Center for American Progress, December 2013.

8. European Commission: Directorate General for Employment, Social Affairs and Inclusion, Unit C3. "Apprentice Supply in the Member States of the European Union." Brussels, Belgium: January 2012. http://ec.europa.eu/social/home.jsp?langId=en.

9. Jacoby, Tamar. "Vocational Education 2.0: Employers Hold the Key to Better Career Training, Civic Report #83." New York City: Manhattan Institute for Policy Research, November 2013.

10. Carlton, Jim, and Caroline Porter. "On a Mission to Save a School: Special Trustee Is Charged with Rescuing One of the Nation's Largest Community Colleges." *The Wall Street Journal* (Tuesday, November 12, 2013): A3. This article discusses the accreditation problems facing the City Colleges of San Francisco caused by budgetary and enrollment issues. It describes the dilemma of no longer being able to serve all community needs.

11. National Center for Educational Statistics. "Fast Facts." http://nces.ed.gov/fastfacts/display.asp?id=40.

12. Cantor, Jeffrey A. "Registered Pre-Apprenticeship: Successful Practices Linking School to Work." *Journal of Industrial Education* 34, no. 3 (1997): 35–58.

13. Ibid.

14. Reed, Dustin. "Why an Apprenticeship Might Be a Faster Ticket to the American Dream Than a College Degree." *PBS Newshour* (June 5, 2014). www.pbs.org/newshour/making-sense/why-an-apprenticeship-may-be-a-faster-ticket-to-the-american-dream-than-a-college-degree/.

15. U.S. Department of Labor, Employment, and Training Administration, Office of Apprenticeship. "Available Occupations." www.doleta.gov/OA/occupations.cfm.

16. Euro-Apprenticeship. www.euroapprenticeship.eu/en/home.html.

17. International Association for the Exchange of Students and Experience. www.iaeste.org.

18. INNSSO (UK) Ltd. "21st Century Apprenticeships: Comparative Review of Apprenticeships in Australia, Canada, Ireland, and the United States, with Reference to the *Richard Review of Apprenticeships* and Implementation in England." London, UK: Federation for Industry Sector Skills and Standards, 2013.

19. Lerman, Robert I. "Training Tomorrow's Workforce: Community Colleges and Apprenticeship as Collaborative Routes to Rewarding Careers." Washington, DC: Center for American Progress, 2009.

20. www.njatc.org.

21. Steedman, Hillary. "Overview of Apprenticeship Systems and Issues: ILO Contribution to the G20 Task Force on Employment." Geneva, Switzerland: International Labour Organization, November 2012.

22. Ibid.

CHAPTER 2

1. Interview by phone with John Ladd, Director U.S. Department of Labor, Office of Apprenticeship, on July 30, 2014. Discussion included business and employer feedback at apprenticeship roundtables conducted by the Department of Labor across the United States during 2014.

2. U.S. Department of Labor, Bureau of Labor Statistics. www.bls.gov.

3. Holzer, Harry J., and Robert I. Lerman. "The Future of Middle-Skill Jobs." *CCF Brief #41* (2009): Washington, DC: Brookings Institution.

4. Virtual Career Network—Healthcare. https://www.vcn.org/health-care/get-qualified/resources/apprenticeship-training.

5. Ibid.

6. Manpower Group. "Talent Survey, 201." www.manpowergroup.us/campaigns/talent-shortage-2013/.

7. Lerman, Robert I. "Training Tomorrow's Workforce: Community Colleges and Apprenticeship as Collaborative Routes to Rewarding Careers." Washington, DC: Center for American Progress, 2009.

8. Jacoby, Tamar. "Vocational Education 2.0: Employers Hold the Key to Better Career Training: Civic Report #83." New York: Manhattan Institute for Policy Research, November 2013.

9. Thornton, Jerry Sue. "The Power of Partnership: Regional Economic Impact through the Joint Apprenticeship Training Committee" (10–13). In *The Role of Community Colleges in Regional Economic Prosperity.* Ann M. Kress and Gerardo E. de los Santos, eds. Phoenix, AZ: The League for Innovation in the Community College, 2014.

10. I first introduced and wrote about these concepts in 1993: Cantor, Jeffrey A. "Apprenticeship and Community Colleges: Promoting Collaboration with Business, Labor and the Community for Workforce Training." Lanham, MD: University Press of America, March 1993.

11. Cantor, Jeffrey A. "Job Training and Economic Development Initiatives: A Study of Potentially Useful Companions." *Educational Evaluation and Policy Analysis* 12, no. 2 (summer 1990): 121–138.

CHAPTER 3

1. World Heritage Foundation. http://worldheritage.org/articles/Holmes_Beckwith.

2. ASTD data for 2012 displaying business expenditures to train employees. www.astd.org/Publications/Magazines/TD/TD-Archive/2012/11/ASTD-2012-State-of-the-Industry-Report.

3. U.S. Department of Labor, Office of Apprenticeship. www.doleta.gov/OA/apprenticeship.cfm.

4. U.S. Department of Labor, Office of Apprenticeship. http://doleta.gov/oa/pdf/brochure.pdf.

5. U.S. Department of Veterans Affairs. www.benefits.va.gov/gibill/docs/factsheets/OJT_Factsheet.pdf.

6. U.S. Department of Veterans Affairs. www.benefits.va.gov/vocrehab/index.asp.

7. Jacoby, Tamar. "Vocational Education 2.0: Employers Hold the Key to Better Career Training, Civic Report No. 83." New York: Manhattan Institute for Policy Research, November 2013.

8. Olinksy, Ben, and Sarah Ayers. "Training for Success: A Policy to Expand Apprenticeships in the United States." Washington, DC: Center for American Progress, December 2013.

9. State of Arkansas, Department of Career Education. http://ace.arkansas.gov/cte/specialPrograms/apprenticeshipAppliedSciences/youthApprenticeship/Pages/taxIncentiveEmployers.aspx.

10. State of Arkansas, Department of Career Education. http://ace.arkansas.gov/cte/specialPrograms/apprenticeshipAppliedSciences/youthApprenticeship/Pages/overview.aspx.

11. U.S. Department of Labor. www.doleta.gov/OA/pdf/funding_fact_sheet.pdf.

12. State of Connecticut, Department of Labor. www.ctdol.state.ct.us/progsupt/appren/taxcr.htm.

13. State of Iowa, Governor. "Iowa 2014 State of Condition of Iowa Address by Terry Branstad, Governor of Iowa." www.governor.iowa.gov/search/apprenticeship.

14. State of Maine, Department of Labor Career Center. http://mainecareercenter.com/services-programs/training/apprenticeship/index.shtml.

15. Maryland Association of Boards of Education. www.mabe.org/wp-content/uploads/2014/04/2014-Leg-Session-Summary.pdf.

16. State of Michigan. www.michigan.gov/documents/school-to-registered_apprenticeship_program_and_tax_credit_5785_7.pdf.

17. State of Missouri, Department of Economic Development—Missouri Works. www.ded.mo.gov/moworks/team-training#training.

18. Rutgers University. "New Jersey's Community Colleges." www.rci.rutgers.edu/~njplace/index.html.

19. State of Rhode Island, Department of Labor and Training. http://dlt.ri.gov/apprenticeship/pdfs/apprentaxcredit.pdf.

20. State of Virginia, Department of Labor. www.doli.virginia.gov/apprenticeship/retraining_taxcredit.html.

21. Lerman, Robert I. "Training Tomorrow's Workforce: Community Colleges and Apprenticeship as Collaborative Routes to Rewarding Careers." Washington, DC: Center for American Progress, December 2009.

22. Smith, Erica. "Australia" (41–51). In *Towards a Model Apprenticeship Framework: A Comparative Analysis of National Apprenticeship Systems*. Geneva, Switzerland: International Labour Organization, 2013.

23. Canada Apprenticeship Forum. caf-fca.org.

24. Canadian Red Seal Trades Program. www.servicecanada.gc.ca/eng/goc/apprenticeship/grants/redseal.shtml.

25. Mentor Works Limited. www.mentorworks.ca/blog/government-funding/government-incentives-for-hiring-training-skilled-workers/.

26. Miller, Linda. "Canada" (52–62). In *Towards a Model Apprenticeship Framework: A Comparative Analysis of National Apprenticeship Systems.* Geneva, Switzerland: International Labour Organization, 2013.

27. Ryan, Paul, and Lorna Unwin. "Apprenticeship in the British 'Training Market.'" *National Institute Economic Review* 178, no. 99 (2001): 99–114.

28. AAT: The Professional Association for Accounting Technicians. www.aat.org.uk/qualifications/apprenticeships-in-england.

29. Miller, Linda. "England" (70–80). In *Towards a Model Apprenticeship Framework: A Comparative Analysis of National Apprenticeship Systems.* Geneva, Switzerland: International Labour Organization, 2013.

30. Saniter, Andreas, and Deitmer Ludger. "Germany" (92–107). In *Towards a Model Apprenticeship Framework: A Comparative Analysis of National Apprenticeship Systems.* Geneva, Switzerland: International Labour Organization, 2013.

31. Attwell, Graham, and Felix Rauner. "Training and Development in Germany." *International Journal of Training and Development* 3, no. 3 (1999): 227–233.

32. Dif, M'Hamed. "France" (81–91). In *Towards a Model Apprenticeship Framework: A Comparative Analysis of National Apprenticeship Systems.* Geneva, Switzerland: International Labour Organization, 2013.

33. International Labour Organization. "Towards a Model Apprenticeship Framework: A Comparative Analysis of National Apprenticeship Systems—Overview of Apprenticeship Systems and Issues." Geneva, Switzerland: ILO contribution to the G20 Task Force on Employment, November 2012.

34. Lerman, *op. cit.*

CHAPTER 4

1. Easton, Nina. "Cool Kids Rule! (And They May Save Detroit)." *Fortune* (June 30, 2014): 60.

2. I am referring to Apprenticeship 2000, Apprenticeship Catawba, and NCTriangle Apprenticeship.

3. Olinsky, Ben, and Sarah Ayres. "Training for Success: A Policy to Expand Apprenticeships in the United States." Washington, DC: Center for American Progress, December 2013.

4. Easton, *op. cit.*

5. Bash, Homa. "Biden Outlines New Apprenticeship Plan for Students." *Medill News Service* (April 7, 2014).

6. Nyhan, Barry. "Chapter 5: Creating the Social Foundation for Apprenticeship in Ireland" (45–58). In *Rediscovering Apprenticeship: Research Findings of the International Network on Innovative Apprenticeship.* Felix Rauner and Erica Smith, eds. Heidelburg, Germany: Springer Publications, 2010.

7. Lerman, Robert I. "Training Tomorrow's Workforce: Community Colleges and Apprenticeship as Collaborative Routes to Rewarding Careers." Washington, DC: Center for American Progress, December 2009.

8. Cantor, Jeffrey A. "Registered Pre-Apprenticeship: Successful Practices Linking School to Work." *Journal of Industrial Education* 34, no. 3 (1997): 35–58.

9. Lerman, Robert I., and Hillard Pouncy. "Why America Should Develop a Youth Apprenticeship System: Policy Report No. 5." Washington, DC: Progressive Policy Institute, March 1990.

10. Nyhan, *op. cit.*

11. U.S. Department of Labor, Employment, and Training Administration, Office of Apprenticeship. "Pre-Apprenticeship Brochure." www.doleta.gov/OA/preapprentice.cfm.

12. Cantor, Jeffrey A. "Registered Pre-Apprenticeship: Successful Practices Linking School to Work." *Journal of Industrial Education* 34, no. 3 (1997): 35–58.

13. The United Association. http://uavip.org/apprenticeships-for-returning-veterans.

14. American Council on Education. www.acenet.edu/higher-education/Pages/Military-Students-and-Veterans.aspx.

15. Goodwill Industries of Washington, DC. www.dcgoodwill.org/docs/PARTFlyer2.09.pdf.

16. Cantor, Jeffrey A. *Cooperative Apprenticeships: A School-to-Work Handbook.* Lancaster, PA: Technomic Publishing Co., 1997.

CHAPTER 5

1. Lerman, Robert, Lauren Eyster, and Kate Chambers. "The Benefits and Challenges of Registered Apprenticeship: The Sponsors' Perspective." Washington, DC: The Urban Institute, March 2009.

2. AMERITECH Die and Mold, Inc. www.amdiemold.com/aboutus.html.

3. Olinsky, Ben, and Sarah Ayres. "Training for Success: A Policy to Expand Apprenticeships in the United States." Washington, DC: Center for American Progress, December 2013.

4. Jacoby, Tamar. "Vocational Education 2.0: Employers Hold the Key to Better Career Training, Civic Report No. 83." New York: Manhattan Institute for Policy Research, November 2013.

5. Interviews were held with firm principals and key managers throughout 2014.

6. Buhler Group AG. "Buhler Apprenticeship Training." Uzwil, Switzerland: September 17, 2014.

7. Lerman, Robert I. "Apprenticeship in the United States." Chapter 11 in *Rediscovering Apprenticeship: Research Findings of the International Network on Innovative Apprenticeship.* Felix Rauner and Erica Smith, eds. Heidelburg, Germany: Springer Publications, 2010.

8. Warwick Institute for Employment Research (2012) in Olinsky and Ayres, *op. cit.*

9. Apprenticeship Carolina. www.apprenticeshipcarolina.com/resources .html.

10. South Carolina Chamber of Commerce. "Apprenticeships in South Carolina: Baseline Report and Recommendations." Columbia, SC: July 2003.

11. Reed, Debbie, Albert Yung-Hsu Liu, Rebecca Kleinman, Annalisa Mastri, Davin Reed, Samina Sattar, and Jessica Ziegler. "An Effectiveness Assessment and Cost-Benefit Analysis of Registered Apprenticeship in 10 States." Oakland, CA: Mathematica Policy Research, July 2012.

12. Lerman, Eyster, and Chambers, *op. cit.*

13. Canadian Federation of Independent Business (CFIB). www.cfib-fcei .ca./cfib-documents/rr3314.pdf.

14. Steedman, Hillary. "Overview of Apprenticeship Systems and Issues: ILO contribution to the G20 Task Force on Employment." Geneva, Switzerland: International Labour Organization, November 2012.

15. As reported by Kathryn Tyler in *HR Magazine* (November 2013): 35.

16. Steedman, *op. cit.*

17. Apprenticeship Carolina. www.apprenticeshipcarolina.com/contactus.html.

18. Cantor, Jeffrey A. "Apprenticeships, Business and Organized Labor, and Community Colleges: Emerging Partnerships." *Journal of Studies in Technical Careers* XIV, no. 2 (1992): 97–114.

19. Cantor, Jeffrey A. "Apprenticeships Link Community—Technical Colleges and Business and Industry for Workforce Training." *Community College Journal of Research and Practice* 19 (1995): 47–71.

CHAPTER 6

1. South Florida Manufacturers' Association Machinist Apprenticeship Program. http://sfma.biz/?page_id=603. Also interviewed the program coordinator on June 24, 2014.

2. Manufacturing Association of South Central Pennsylvania. www .mascpa.org/workforcedevelopment.html. Interviewed apprenticeship program coordinator on June 23, 2014, by telephone.

3. Telephone interviews were held with representatives of both of the trade associations during spring 2014.

4. National Automobile Dealers' Association. www.nada.org.

5. Telephone interview with Mr. Gerald Murphy, former CEO of Washington Area New Automobile Dealers Association, July 2, 2014. Also see www .adei-programs.org/Students.cfm.

6. Automobile Dealer Education Institute. www.adei-programs.org.

7. Interview with Walter Siegenthaler, cofounder of Apprenticeship 2000, executive vice president of Daetwyler USA, and chair of the North Carolina Apprenticeship Council, July 9, 2014. Consortium web page at http://apprent iceship2000.com/index.html.

8. Telephone interview with Michigan Economic Development Corporation staff, August 18, 2014.

9. On-site visit, South Carolina Technical College System, and interviews with SCTCS and state economic development staff, September 3, 2014.

10. Ivy Tech Community College. www.ivytech.edu/academics/apprentice ships.html.

11. Thornton, Jerry Sue. "The Power of Partnership: Regional Economic Impact through the Joint Apprenticeship Training Committee" (10–13). In *the Role of Community Colleges in Regional Economic Prosperity*. Ann M. Kress and Gerardo E. de los Santos, eds. Phoenix, AZ: The League for Innovation in the Community College, 2014.

12. College of Southern Nevada. www.csn.edu/pages/3683.asp.

13. The Electrical Training Alliance. www.njatc.org/training/credit.aspx.

14. California Fire Fighter Joint Apprenticeship Committee. www.cffjac .org/go/jac/about-jac/.

15. California Apprenticeship Coordinators Association. www.calapprent iceship.org/faqs.php#costs.

16. Gloucester County Workforce Investment Board. http://gloucester-local .civicasoft.com/depts/w/wib/about/committees/appwd.asp.

17. State of California, Labor and Workforce Development Agency. www .cwib.ca.gov/res/docs/state_plans/Final%20Approved%20State%20Plan/ Appendix%20N%20Joint%20Letter%20to%20LWIBs%20on%20RAPs.pdf.

18. Stieritz, Ann Marie. "Apprenticeship Carolina: Building a 21st Century Workforce through Statewide Collaboration." *Community College Journal of Research and Practice* 33 (2009): 980–982.

19. U.S. Department of Labor. "Investing in Apprenticeships." *The DOL Newsletter*, December 11, 2014.

20. NJPlace. www.njplace.com. State of New Jersey did not refund project; now redirects to www.rci.rutgers.edu/~njplace/.

CHAPTER 7

1. Cantor, Jeffrey A. "Occupational Education, Economic Development, and the Role of the Community College." *Journal of Studies in Technical Careers* XII, no. 4 (fall 1990): 313–326.

2. Thornton, Jerry Sue. "The Power of Partnership: Regional Economic Impact through the Joint Apprenticeship Training Committee" (10–13). In *The Role of Community Colleges in Regional Economic Prosperity*. Ann M. Kress and Gerardo E. de los Santos, eds. Phoenix, AZ: The League for Innovation in the Community College, 2014.

3. Cantor, Jeffrey A. "Effective Advisory Committees: Strategies for Success." Invited presentation to the Fire and Emergency Services Higher Education Conference. Emmitsburg, MD: U.S. Fire Administration, National Fire Academy, June 2002 and June 2004.

4. Lerman, Robert, Lauren Eyster, and Kate Chambers. "The Benefits and Challenges of Registered Apprenticeship: The Sponsors' Perspective." Washington, DC: The Urban Institute, March 2009.

5. Electrical Training Alliance. www.njatc.org.

6. College Board. http://accuplacer.collegeboard.org/students.

7. Candidate Physical Ability Test. www.nipsta.org/cpat/.

8. Riverside Community College (CA). www.mvcsp.com/law/Testing%20%20Orientations/Physical%20Fitness%20Assessment.aspx.

9. Lerman, Eyster, and Chambers, *op. cit.*

10. American Council on Education. www.acenet.edu/higher-education/topics/Pages/Prior-Learning-Assessments.aspx.

11. National Occupational Competency Testing Institute. www.nocti.org.

12. Florida Department of Education, Division of Workforce Education. www.fldoe.org/workforce/dwdframe/law_cluster_frame14.asp.

13. National Center for Construction Education and Research. www.nccer.org/uploads/fileLibrary/C-IM%20Mechanic.pdf.

14. Electrical Training Alliance. http://nti.njatc.org/training.aspx.

15. Gonzalez, Jenifer. "Apprenticeship Programs Expand with Help of Community Colleges." *TECH Directions* 70, no. 9 (April 2011): 31–33.

16. Ibid.

17. Central Piedmont Community College, Apprenticeship 2000. www.cpcc.edu/et/apprenticeships/new_appren.

18. Catawba Valley Community College. www.cvcc.edu/Workforce_Development/Apprenticeship_Catawba.cfm.

19. Stieritz, Ann Marie. "Apprenticeship Carolina: Building a 21st Century Workforce through Statewide Collaboration." *Community College Journal of Research and Practice* 33 (2009): 980–982.

20. Bates Technical College. www.bates.ctc.edu/apprenticeship.

21. South Seattle Community College. http://georgetown.southseattle.edu/AEC/aboutapprenticeships.aspx.

22. Newport News Shipbuilding Apprentice School. www.as.edu.

CHAPTER 8

1. Ayres, Sarah. "National Standards for Strong Apprenticeships." Washington, DC: Center for American Progress, December 2014.

2. Evans, Neil. "Information Technology Jobs and Skill Standards." Chapter 2 in *Technology Everywhere: A Campus Agenda for Educating and Managing Workers in the Digital Age*, Brian L. Hawkins, Julia A. Rudy, and William H. Wallace Jr., eds. Washington, DC: EDUCAUSE, 2002.

3. National Workforce Center for Emerging Technologies. www.tssb.org/sites/default/files/wwwpages/repos/pdfiles/NWCETSkillStandards03.pdf.

4. The National Skills Standards Project. http://www2.ed.gov/offices/OVAE/OccSkills/pubrev2.pdf.

5. U.S. Department of Labor, Employment, and Training Administration. http://wdr.doleta.gov/opr/fulltext/95-voluntary.pdf.

6. Lake Washington Technical College. www.tssb.org/sites/default/files/wwwpages/repos/pdfiles/gamecontent.pdf.

7. Jacoby, Tamar. "Vocational Education 2.0: Employers Hold the Key to Better Career Training, Civic Report #83." New York: Manhattan Institute for Policy Research, November 2013.

8. National Center for Construction Education and Research. www.nccer.org/missionvision.

9. National Institute for Metalworking Skills, Inc. https://www.nims-skills.org/web/nims/home.

10. National Workforce Center for Technologies. www.tssb.org/sites/default/files/wwwpages/repos/pdfiles/NWCETSkillStandards03.pdf.

11. National Registry of Emergency Medical Technicians. https://www.nremt.org/nremt/about/nremt_history.asp.

12. UK Conservative Party. "Building Skills, Transforming Lives: A Training and Apprenticeships Revolution: Opportunity Agenda Policy Green Paper No. 7." London, UK: UK Conservative Party, n.d.

13. Toronto Workforce Innovation Group. www.workforceinnovation.ca/sites/default/files/Sector%20Council%20Information%20for%20Employers.pdf.

14. Cantor, Jeffrey A. "Skills Certifications and Workforce Development: Partnering with Industry and Ourselves." *Leadership Abstracts* 15, no. 1 (January 2002). Phoenix, AZ: League for Innovation in the Community College.

15. Jacoby, *op. cit.*

16. American Council on Education. www.acenet.edu/news-room/Pages/College-Credit-Recommendation-Service-CREDIT.aspx.

17. Thomas Edison State College. www.tesc.edu/partners/Organization-Training.cfm.

18. Charter Oak State College. www.charteroak.edu/prior-learning-assessment/.

19. NJPlace. www.njplace.com. Now redirects to http://ucc.rutgers.edu/nj-place.

20. As reported in *TIME* Magazine (June 2, 2014): 5.

CHAPTER 10

1. www.advantageoakland.com/workforce/Pages/workJobTrainandEd.aspx.

2. www.cael.org.

3. www.learningcounts.org.

4. http://nocti.org.

5. www.nawb.org.

Bibliography

American Council on Education. (n.d.) "National Guide to College Credit for Workforce Training." www.acenet.edu/news-room/Pages/National-Guide -to-College-Credit-for-Workforce-Training.aspx.

Attwell, Graham, and Felix Rauner. (1999). "Training and Development in Germany." *International Journal of Training and Development* 3, no. 3 (September): 227–233.

Ayres, Sarah. (December 2014). "National Standards for Strong Apprenticeships" (Washington, DC: Center for American Progress).

Bash, Homa. (April 7, 2014). "Biden Outlines New Apprenticeship Plan for Students." Medill News Service.

Buhler Group AG. (September 17, 2014). *Buhler Apprenticeship Training.* Uzwil, Switzerland.

Buhler Group AG. (2014). *ClassUnlimited Project.* Uzwil, Switzerland.

Cantor, Jeffrey A. (2006). "Lifelong Learning and the Academy: The Changing Nature of Professional Continuing Education." *ASHE–ERIC Higher Education Report* 32, no. 2. San Francisco: Jossey-Bass Higher Education Series.

Cantor, Jeffrey A. (2002). "Skills Certifications and Workforce Development: Partnering with Industry and Ourselves." Phoenix AZ: League for Innovation in the Community College. *Leadership Abstracts* 15, no. 1 (January).

Cantor, Jeffrey A. (June 2002/June 2004). "Effective Advisory Committees: Strategies for Success." Invited paper presentation to the Fire and Emergency Services Higher Education Conference, U.S. Fire Administration, National Fire Academy, Emmitsburg, MD.

Cantor, Jeffrey A. (1997). *Cooperative Apprenticeships: A School-to-Work Handbook.* Lancaster, PA: Technomic Publishing Co.

Cantor, Jeffrey A. (1997). "Registered Pre-Apprenticeship: Successful Practices Linking School to Work." *Journal of Industrial Education* 34, no. 3: 35–58.

Cantor, Jeffrey A. (1995). "Apprenticeships Link Community–Technical Colleges and Business and Industry for Workforce Training." *Community College Journal of Research and Practice* 19: 47–71.

Cantor, Jeffrey A. (1993). *Apprenticeship and Community Colleges—Collaborations for Tomorrow's Workforce.* Lanham, MD: University Press of America.

Cantor, Jeffrey A. (1992). "Apprenticeships, Business and Organized Labor, and Community Colleges: Emerging Partnerships." *Journal of Studies in Technical Careers,* XIV no. 2: 97–114.

Cantor, Jeffrey A. (1990). "Occupational Education, Economic Development, and the Role of the Community College." *Journal of Studies in Technical Careers* XII, no. 4 (fall): 313–326.

Cantor, Jeffrey A., "Job Training and Economic Development Initiatives: A Study of Potentially Useful Companions." *Educational Evaluation and Policy Analysis,* 12 no. 2 (summer 1990): 121–138.

Carlton, Jim, and Caroline Porter. (2013). "On a Mission to Save a School: Special Trustee Is Charged with Rescuing One of the Nation's Largest Community Colleges." *The Wall Street Journal,* November 12, p. A3.

Cuyahoga Community College. (June 11, 2014). *Construction Apprenticeship Brochure.* http://tri-c.edu/workforce/Construction/Documents/Apprentice_WEB.pdf.

Dif, M'Hamed. (2013). *Toward a Model Apprenticeship Framework: A Comparative Analysis of National Apprenticeship Systems.* New Delhi, India: International Labor Organization, The World Bank.

Easton, Nina. (2014). Cool Kids Rule! (and They May Save Detroit). *Fortune,* June 30, p. 60.

European Commission, Directorate General for Employment, Social Affairs and Inclusion, Unit C-3. (January 2012). *Apprenticeship Supply in the Member States of the European Union: Executive Summary.* Brussels, Belgium: European Union.

Evans, Neil. (2002). *Technology Everywhere: A Campus Agenda for Educating and Managing Workers in the Digital Age*; chapter 2, "Information Technology Jobs and Skill Standards." San Francisco: Jossey-Bass.

Fuller, Alison, and Lorna Unwin. (2012). "What's the Point of Adult Apprenticeships?" *Adult Learning* (spring): 8–14.

Fuller, Allison, and Lorna Unwin. (2012). "The Great Skills Debate." *Training Journal.com* (August): 12–14.

Gonzalez, Jenifer. (2011). "Apprenticeship Programs Expand with Help of Community Colleges." *TECH Directions* 70, no. 9 (April): 31–33.

Holzer, Harry J., and Robert I. Lerman. "The Future of Middle-Skill Jobs." *CCF Brief #41* (2009). Washington, DC: Brookings Institution.

International Labor Organization and the World Bank. (2013). *Towards a Model Apprenticeship Framework: A Comparative Analysis of National Apprenticeship Systems.* Bangkok, Thailand: The World Bank.

INNSSO (UK) Ltd. (2013). *21st Century Apprenticeships: Comparative Review of Apprenticeships in Australia, Canada, Ireland, and the United States, with Reference to the Richard Review of Apprenticeships and Implementation in England.* London: Federation for Industry Sector Skills and Standards.

Jacoby, Tamar. (November 2013). Civic Report #8: "Vocational Education 2.0: Employers Hold the Key to Better Career Training." New York: Manhattan Institute for Policy Research.

Lerman, Robert I., and Hillard Pouncy. (March 1990). "Why America Should Develop a Youth Apprenticeship System—Policy Report No. 5." Washington, DC: Progressive Policy Institute.

Lerman, Robert I. (2009). "Training Tomorrow's Workforce: Community Colleges and Apprenticeship as Collaborative Routes to Rewarding Careers." Washington, DC: Center for American Progress.

Lerman, Robert, Lauren Eyster, and Kate Chambers. "The Benefits and Challenges of Registered Apprenticeship: The Sponsors' Perspective." (March 2009): Washington, DC: The Urban Institute.

Lerman, Robert I. (2010). "Apprenticeship in the United States." Chapter 11 in *Rediscovering Apprenticeship: Research Findings of the International Network on Innovative Apprenticeship*, eds. Felix Rauner and Erica Smith. Heidelburg, Germany: Springer Publications.

Nyhan, Barry. (2010). "Creating the Social Foundation for Apprenticeship in Ireland." Chapter 5 in *Rediscovering Apprenticeship: Research Findings of the International Network on Innovative Apprenticeship*, eds. Felix Rauner and Erica Smith. Heidelburg, Germany: Springer Publications.

Olinsky, Ben, and Sarah Ayres. (December 2013). "Training for Success: A Policy to Expand Apprenticeships in the United States." Washington, DC: Center for American Progress.

Ryan, Paul, and Lorna Unwin. (2001). "Apprenticeship in the British 'Training Market.'" *National Institute Economic Review*. London, England: National Institute of Economic and Social Research.

Saniter, Andreas, and Ludger Deitmer. (2013). *Toward a Model Apprenticeship Framework: A Comparative Analysis of National Apprenticeship Systems.* New Delhi, India: International Labor Organization and the World Bank.

South Carolina Chamber of Commerce. (July 2003). *Apprenticeships in South Carolina: Baseline Report and Recommendations.* Columbia, SC.

Steedman, Hillary. (November 2012). "Overview of Apprenticeship Systems and Issues: ILO Contribution to the G20 Task Force on Employment." Geneva, Switzerland: International Labor Organization.

Stieritz, Ann Marie. (2009). "Apprenticeship Carolina: Building a 21st Century Workforce Through Statewide Collaboration." *Community College Journal of Research and Practice* 33: 980–982.

Swiss Confederation, Federal Department of Economic Affairs. (2013). *Vocational and Professional Education and Training in Switzerland.* Bern, Switzerland.

Swiss Confederation, Federal Department of Economic Affairs. (2012). *Entering the Labour Market: Report on Measures to Ease the Transition to Upper-Secondary Level.* Bern, Switzerland.

Thornton, Jerry Sue. (2014). "The Power of Partnership: Regional Economic Impact through the Joint Apprenticeship Training Committee" (pp. 10–13). In *The Role of Community Colleges in Regional Economic Prosperity*, eds. Ann M. Kress and Gerardo E. de los Santos. Phoenix, AZ: The League for Innovation in the Community College.

UK Conservative Party. (n.d.) "Building Skills, Transforming Lives: A Training and Apprenticeships Revolution." *Opportunity Agenda Policy Green Paper No. 7.* London.

U.S. Department of Labor, Employment and Training Administration, Office of Apprenticeship. "Available Occupations." www.doleta.gov/OA/occupations.cfm.

U.S. Department of Labor, Employment and Training Administration, Office of Apprenticeship. "Pre-Apprenticeship Brochure." www.doleta.gov/OA/preapprentice.cfm.

The World Bank. (2013). "Toward a Model Apprenticeship Framework: A Comparative Analysis of National Apprenticeship Systems." New Delhi, India: International Labor Organization.

Index